The Common Market
The European Community in Action

by J. WARREN NYSTROM
and PETER MALOF

Linda E. Connors
1965

A SEARCHLIGHT ORIGINAL
under the general editorship of

GEORGE W. HOFFMAN
University of Texas

G. ETZEL PEARCY
*United States
Department of State*

D. VAN NOSTRAND COMPANY, INC.

PRINCETON, NEW JERSEY

TORONTO   LONDON

NEW YORK

Preface

This book presents a synthesis of authoritative materials and insights on Western Europe's efforts, since World War II, to create a unified and progressive community of nations. The literature on the subject, particularly its economic aspects, is extensive. Yet relatively little has been done thus far to help the nonspecialist reader grasp the broad significance of the movement toward European unity—one of the most important political developments of our century. The perspective and analysis provided in the pages that follow should help fill this gap.

Western Europe's search for new forms of integration has wide-ranging implications for its role in the free-world struggle with the communist bloc, for the continued solidarity of the Western alliance, and for the evolution of new patterns of international economic and political relations that can meet the realities of an increasingly interdependent globe. Ravaged as never before, the region revived after World War II in a phenomenal renaissance of economic growth and technological progress. Today, despite powerful divisive forces, the nations of Western Europe are forging a new partnership in consultation and action.

This dynamic resurgence, greatly stimulated by American aid, represents a major defeat for postwar Soviet policy and now looms as a serious threat to continuing Soviet ambitions in Eastern Europe and in the Continent as a whole. At the same time, however, the remarkable restoration of West European power confronts the United States with the prospect of a major foreign policy dilemma. The United States since the war has exerted great energy and initiative in supporting Western Europe's striving toward integration. It has also sought to strengthen broader transatlantic and free-

3

world ties. These twin American objectives are coming increasingly into conflict.

Creating a new sense of self-reliance on the Continent, the West European movement toward economic and political unity has produced growing pressures for a greater measure of European independence in world affairs. The region's new-found sense of power is giving rise to controversies within the Western alliance and could, in the long run, divide the United States from its most important treaty partners. Disagreements within the Western camp are tempered, however, by a common realization that Europe and the United States, together as equals, can more than meet the threats emanating from the Soviet world.

Neither the United States nor Western Europe can stem the communist tide alone. Even if the United States could preserve its territorial security exclusively by forces based in the Western Hemisphere, a communist occupation of Western Europe would constitute a major global defeat. Western Europe's security, in turn, is dependent on continued solidarity with the United States. Combined, the two regions possess an expanding industrial base which can counter the full range of political, military and economic challenges likely to be posed by the Soviet Union through the next decade.

Beyond the Cold War, the process of Western Europe's integration is contributing to a dispersion of world power which is potentially of decisive importance to the free world in its search for a more stable international order. Even as Western Europe becomes less responsive to American power and influence, it is testing and developing new techniques and institutions for moderating international rivalries and conflicts. This great human experiment is helping to create new international forms that are not only reshaping the modern world, but offering some hope for the perpetuation of its civilization.

J. WARREN NYSTROM
PETER MALOF

Washington, D.C.
August 1, 1962

Contents

I   *Europe in Flux*

C̲LEFT by two gigantic power blocs, the face of Europe today presents a kaleidoscope of centripetal and centrifugal forces that are re-shaping the organization of the Continent. This transformation, perhaps the most significant international development of our time, is profoundly changing the character of global economic and political relationships.

PERSPECTIVE

Each half of the Continent—communist and non-communist—has embarked on a critical experiment in regional unity. The Sovietization of Eastern Europe, generated by the requirements of Russian power, is rapidly destroying the region's potential for indigenous cohesion or independent growth. The present integration of Western Europe, in contrast, derives its impetus from the inexorable interdependence of free nations and is strengthening the area's capacity to act as an independent center of power. Both regions are seeking to overcome deep-seated divisions rooted in discordant national drives and aspirations. Yet each is pursuing a separate internal development which promises to perpetuate the fundamental division of Europe as a whole.

Russia's European satellites are well along the road to complete integration. Through a Council for Mutual Economic Assistance (known as COMECON)[1], the Soviet Union is welding Eastern Europe into one powerful and coordinated industrial community.

---

[1] Members: Albania, Bulgaria, Czechoslovakia, East Germany, Hungary, Poland, Rumania, Soviet Union. Observers: Red China, North Korea, North Vietnam, Outer Mongolia. Albania, intransigent and ostracized, occupies a uniquely ambiguous position in the bloc.

It has taken pains, however, to link the satellites individually with its own economic and political life, requiring each to limit its production to relatively narrow specialties specified by Moscow. The scope for multi-lateral cooperation and association in Eastern Europe is severely restricted and controlled to reinforce the separate dependence of the satellites on the USSR. The region's unitary yet brittle structure is sustained primarily by the pervasive presence of external power.

While absorbed into the Soviet power complex, Eastern Europe remains permeated with cross-currents of intermittent and repressed ferment. Nationalistic pressures continue to test the process of Sovietization as well as to strain the developing relations between communist regimes. The Soviet Union has been groping, in recent years, for more flexible and efficient administrative forms so as to reduce its reliance on naked force as an instrument of control, to appease and harness national grievances, and to render its domination more effective. Tensions released by this effort could again, as in 1956, fracture the monolithic façade of the satellite bloc, but are unlikely to break the mold of communist hegemony imposed at the close of World War II.

The enormous strategic, material, and political advantages which the Soviet Union obtains from this hegemony far outweigh the burden of controlling dissident nationalities and amalgamating their disparate economies. Communist control of the region, and particularly of East Germany, provides the Soviet Union with considerable leverage for undermining both the NATO structure and Western Europe's indigenous strivings for unity. Barring a drastic reversal in Soviet policy, the Soviet regime can be expected to press these advantages as long as it remains in control of a viable and resilient system of power.

Western Europe, the focus of this book, is the mainspring of the most volatile and dynamic forces for change now sweeping the Continent. These forces acquired form as the nations of Western Europe, emerging from the crucible of war, prepared themselves for the throes of recovery. Sir Winston Churchill's dramatic appeal, in the spring of 1948, for some form of political union released a wave of enthusiasm for visionary plans. Fear of expanding Soviet power gave this "European movement" much of its impetus. As Paul-Henri Spaak later observed: "The European nations are somewhat like scattered chicks. When they see a hawk hovering above them . . . they tend to come together."

Blending with the fear, however, were many other emotions and motives: a sense of common misfortune resulting from political rivalries and economic divisions; a resolve that Europe must never again experience the horrors of internecine strife; a reawakened pride in the European heritage; a conviction that national foundations were too narrow to assure the revival of European civilization; a hope for rapid economic and social progress through Europe-wide cooperation and association; a desire to create some kind of a "third force" to counter both Russian and American dominance; a determination to work for a fuller share of responsibilities in world affairs, either independently or as a genuine ally and equal partner in the Atlantic Alliance.

Many idealistic projects looking toward some sort of political federation were put forward and aroused, initially, considerable ardor. Soon, however, exponents of skepticism and doubt helped to darken the glow of enthusiasm. In the cold light of day, it seemed inconceivable that the citizens of individual countries, with strong national attachments, would readily sweep aside age-old practices and beliefs—economic, political, social—for the sake of utopian paper plans drafted by intellectuals. Nevertheless, as various statesmen, politicians, and intellectual leaders began to apply their energies to the arduous task of sorting out the wheat of the practicable from the chaff of the visionary, the concept of Western European unity survived as the one great creative political idea to emerge out of the postwar era.

Subtle differences between Continental and British attitudes, however, deeply colored the drive for greater cohesion in the years that followed. On the Continent, a loss of faith in existing political institutions spurred a search for new political and economic forms that could inspire confidence and loyalty. Britain, preserving much of the strength of its traditional institutions, did not feel as urgent a need for new European institutions. This difference contributed to the development of diverse, in some cases radically different, approaches to the problems of association and unity.

The tension between vision and reality remained a continuing and powerful force in Western Europe's resurgence and subsequent transformation. Precedent-shattering strides toward closer unity were taken—but in regional fragments of varying importance and strength that perpetuated as much as resolved strong national differences. Rivalries persisted both within and between the new regional groupings and entities that gradually assumed shape.

Thus the "European movement" has conformed neither to the dreams of the "visionaries" nor to the expectations of the "realists." Individual national aspirations and ambitions are not losing their political potency. On the other hand, revolutionary new forms of regional consultation, coordination, and unity, for the time being clothed with economic meaning, are being forged. But their great significance lies in foreshadowing not the elimination of conflicts among nations but the unexpected evolution of a new system of international relations for controlling such conflicts.

WESTERN EUROPE SINCE THE WAR

The present organization of Western Europe (see Figure 1) embraces a bewildering number of separate intergovernmental, supranational, political, economic, social, religious, educational, cultural, professional, and other groupings. The more important of these include:

(1) the North Atlantic Treaty Organization (NATO), an extension of the wartime alliance re-fashioned to meet the Soviet military threat;

(2) the Western European Union (WEU), seeking to strengthen peace and security among member states through agreements on arms control;

(3) the Council of Europe (CE), endeavoring to build greater

The ORGANIZATION of WESTERN EUROPE, 1961

Organization for Economic Cooperation and Development (OECD)
(INCLUDES CANADA and the UNITED STATES)

European Free Trade Association (EFTA)

KEY

→ Denotes Membership

---→ Denotes Association

European Economic Community (COMMON MARKET)
European Atomic Energy Community (EURATOM)
European Coal and Steel Community (ECSC)

Benelux

The Council of Europe (CE)

North Atlantic Treaty Organization (NATO)
(INCLUDES CANADA and the UNITED STATES)

Western European Union (WEU)

IRELAND | ICELAND | TURKEY | GREECE | ITALY | FRANCE | WEST GERMANY | BELGIUM | LUXEMBOURG | NETHERLANDS | UNITED KINGDOM | DENMARK | NORWAY | PORTUGAL | AUSTRIA | SWEDEN | SWITZERLAND | SPAIN | FINLAND unity among its members on the basis of the ideals and principles which are their common heritage;

(4) Benelux, working to strengthen the economic union between Belgium, the Netherlands, and Luxembourg;

(5) the European Coal and Steel Community (ECSC), administering a common market for coal and steel among member countries;

(6) the European Atomic Energy Community (Euratom), responsible for developing nuclear research and for creating a common market in nuclear industry;

(7) the European Economic Community or Common Market (EEC or CM), working to achieve a high degree of both economic and political unity;

(8) the European Free Trade Association (EFTA), formed to establish a free trade area which would preserve the internal autonomy of member countries; and

(9) the Organization for Economic Cooperation and Development (OECD), formed on American initiative as a successor to the Organization for European Economic Cooperation (OEEC) to enable member countries to harmonize their economic policies for both their own interests and the broader interests of the free world.

To place this fragmented structure into perspective, a brief review of Western Europe's postwar history may be helpful. Four major problems confronted the West at the end of World War II: the rebuilding of war-torn economies; the growing threat of Soviet power; the reintegration of Germany into the democratic European community; and the restoration of Europe's position in the world on a new and more viable foundation.

As has been indicated, the experience of two world wars had persuaded many European leaders that only a less divisive, more cohesive Europe could assure the Continent's survival, revival, and growth. Some were convinced that traditional state systems and concepts of sovereignty had become obsolete and required re-definition in the face of mid-twentieth-century realities. Others—particularly government officials and administrators, industrial entrepre-

neurs and managers, and labor leaders—responded to the revolutionary impact of science and technology on the traditional patterns
of European economic and social life. For them, the breakdown of
restrictive national borders and autarchic economic systems was
necessary not for political reasons but in order to meet the practical
demands of industrial progress, mechanized mass-production, and
standardization in the habits and tastes of diverse peoples.

Strong American support for European integration acted as a
major catalyst in galvanizing specific action. In 1947, the United
States offered massive aid under the Marshall Plan on condition
that European countries chart the outlines of their rehabilitation.
This dramatic and historic initiative prompted 14 European countries to form the Organization for European Economic Cooperation (OEEC) for the purpose of administering Marshall Plan aid
and pioneering in economic cooperation. The OEEC, eventually
embracing 18 European states, served as a vital forum for frank discussions of mutual problems and policies. In gathering facts, coordinating data and programs, and studying new problems as they
arose—in trade liberalization, monetary stabilization, and convertibility—it helped build a significant body of traditions and habits in
day-to-day international consultation.

In response to the rapid expansion of Soviet power and pressure,
the North Atlantic Treaty Organization, eventually composing 15
members, was established in April 1949 both as a defensive military
alliance and as a potential mechanism for developing political, economic, social, and cultural cooperation among member countries.
The United States, the prime mover behind NATO, also continued to offer consistent support and encouragement to the concept
of joint action by European nations in order to benefit from the advantages of a large single market comparable to its own. The Economic Cooperation Act of 1949 declared it to be United States policy to encourage Western European unification.

American policymakers, however, soon encountered considerable
difficulty in agreeing on how this objective should be defined. In
consequence, European advocates of union found occasion to criti-

cize the United States for lacking vigor in its support of the unification idea. Part of the difficulty lay in the fact that Europeans themselves were unable to agree on the basis of unity—geographic, cultural or spiritual, economic, political, or strategic—or on the meaning of the term "Europe." As different groups embraced the concept of unity for different purposes, the United States occasionally found itself supporting different and conflicting approaches to integration.

THE SEARCH FOR REGIONAL COHESION

Contradictions in basic outlooks and objectives spawned a proliferation of private and public groups and organizations which robbed the European movement of central direction. National and ideological diversity was reflected in the basic attitudes of leading champions of political integration—Conservatives such as Winston Churchill, Christian Democrats such as Robert Schuman and Konrad Adenauer, and Socialists such as Paul-Henri Spaak. Lacking a coherent expression of purpose and objectives, the movement found itself channeled into slow functional, rather than political, integration. Officials and administrators preoccupied with the problems of efficient economic management and growth—emerging as a new European "power elite"—provided the major stimulus for schemes of economic unity. The drive for political integration waxed and waned, depending upon the ebb and flow of Soviet pressure.

In 1949, France and Italy made an abortive attempt to form a customs union. The European Coal and Steel Community—composed of the present members of the Common Market—was established in 1951. Building on a tradition established by the Belgium-Luxembourg customs union (formed in 1921 and enlarged by the addition of the Netherlands in 1944), the common market in coal and steel served as a highly successful pilot project in economic integration. More than a common market, the ECSC levied its own taxes, though its supranational powers were carefully limited by the member governments in practice.

These and other efforts at closer integration suffered a setback in

1954, when the French Assembly rejected a treaty which would have established a European Defense Community: an ambitious military and political supranational institution. The treaty, the result of a proposal by M. Rene Pleven in 1950, had been signed by France, Germany, Italy, and Benelux in 1952. Its rejection led to the formation of the Western European Union to salvage some of the work that had gone into the defense community proposal.

Suffering a major defeat, despite the creation of the Western European Union, proponents of unity now confronted a renewed emphasis on national sovereignty and self-interest in Western European relations. This development was traceable to several factors: a feeling of new confidence accompanying Europe's economic recovery; a lessened fear of Soviet military aggression after the death of Stalin; growing preoccupations, especially by France, with extra-European affairs; and emerging disagreements over the decision-making processes of the Atlantic Alliance with the advent of a new nuclear weapons technology.

Manifestations of nationalism and distrust found expression in a variety of intergovernmental relationships: Austro-Italian conflicts over South Tyrol; irredentist strivings in West Germany; British-Icelandic fisheries disputes; tendencies in Britain to revert to a traditional pattern of "splendid isolation"; Gaullism in France as a call for a revival of national greatness; friction between Britain and the Franco-German bloc over the military and economic organization of Europe.

The resurgence of nationalism, however, differed significantly from the exclusive chauvinism which marked Europe in the late 19th century. National rivalries expressed themselves largely within the framework of the Atlantic Alliance and its inescapable worldwide commitments. General acceptance of the partnership of the West defined the limits of national ambitions, which no longer encompassed national power *per se* but a demand for equality in the partnership and a voice in the shaping of Western Europe as a whole. The demand for equality reflected considerable resentment, if not rejection, of United States leadership, and this attitude had the effect of deflecting some of the pressures for European unity toward neutralism or the creation of a third force.

Neutralist currents of opinion composed a diverse mixture of conflicting drives, attitudes, and emotions. In part, they reflected a defensive reaction to the alleged contaminating influence of American mass culture attending the democratization of European society—the opening of educational opportunities and raising of working-class living standards. The basic sources of neutralist sentiment, however, were imbedded in the fears, resentments, and suspicions generated by the Cold War.

Many Europeans felt that they would be forced to bear the brunt of any nuclear holocaust. Neutralism offered some hope of escaping the omnipresent risks of nuclear conflict and expressed itself in various forms: reactions against the establishment of United States missile bases on European soil; ban-the-bomb campaigns; opposition to rearmament in Western Germany. The fear psychosis, effectively stimulated by Soviet psychological pressures, sometimes led to defeatism, a belief that the West would not be able to avert disaster in the face of rapid Soviet technological advances. Lack of confidence in United States policy, often depicted as swayed by mass hysteria and addicted to "brinkmanship," contributed to defeatist or neutralist feelings.

As a form of European neutralism, the "third force" concept appealed to two additional emotions: a belief that both the American and Soviet ways of life represented basically similar materialistic interests; and a hope that a strong and united Europe would mediate between the two superpowers to preserve peace. The "third force" movement, a Continental equivalent to nationalism, lacked organized form and to some extent was restrained by the realization, on the part of responsible European leaders, that Western Europe's survival hinged in the last analysis on the nuclear power of the United States.

Armed with this sober assessment of Western Europe's vulnerability, the foreign ministers of the European Coal and Steel Community quietly pursued their consideration of further steps toward integration. In April 1956, they finally agreed to draft treaties for a common market and an atomic energy community. Both treaties were signed in Rome on March 25, 1957, and came into effect on January 1, 1958, establishing the European Economic Community (EEC) and Euratom. Six Continental nations were now bound together in three distinct but interlocking communities.

This process of functional integration did less to produce unity —in the sense of a continuous state of harmony and accord with respect to policy and action—than to contribute to the fragmentation of parts of the European whole. Within the new semi-supranational institutions of the Six—which possessed the potential for political integration—national conflicts persisted in finding expression. To outsiders, the integration of the Six seemed to present the threat of an exclusive Continental unity which could undermine the establishment of a more broadly based community.

Throughout 1957 and 1958, the Six of the new Common Market and the remaining 12 nations of OEEC made herculean efforts to reach an understanding on their common future. Some countries favored the creation of a large free trade area rather than a closely integrated union of European states. Great Britain, in particular, felt that its interests outside Europe were as strong as, if not stronger than, those in Europe. On the other hand, French-German desires for a lasting rapprochement which would exorcise their historic enmity buttressed Continental opposition to a loose European grouping with limited commitments.

The discussions dramatized the depth of Western Europe's divisions. A basic cleavage separated those who favored a pragmatic, step-by-step approach to the problem of cooperation and those who insisted on more binding institutional arrangements. Focusing on short-term trading difficulties, Britain preferred to establish a free trade area, rather than a customs union as envisaged in the Common Market, which would preserve unilateral external tariff arrangements. It considered a common external tariff discriminatory to outsiders and opposed the institutional harmonization of social and economic policies as a threat to its sovereignty.

British leaders had been slow to recognize the ideal of European integration as a practical possibility. With the failure of the European Defense Community fresh in mind, they were sure that Europe was not ready for any surrender of sovereignty and labeled as visionary any formal structure of integration. As it became evident that the Continental nations were determined to build a new basis for unity, the United Kingdom worked hard to sell its own vision of a European free trade area. In the British view, flexible and pragmatic arrangements would permit the evolution of a system of laws built on cases as opposed to an "artificial" code as developed by theorists and logicians. The free trade area would not require any surrender of sovereignty and at the same time would preserve British Continental markets, relieve Commonwealth apprehensions, and enhance Britain's influence in Europe.

The United Kingdom nurtured high hopes for the free trade area until the fall of 1958. It believed it could muster French endorsement of the concept, at least in principle, and count on substantial support from both Germany and the United States. It underestimated both the dynamism of Continental developments and the enthusiasm of American policy for rapid progress toward a strong and united Europe.

Months of negotiation for a broad agreement among all the OEEC countries ended in failure. France, under the new leadership of General de Gaulle, continued to support the Common Market concept. Both de Gaulle and Dr. Adenauer publicly affirmed their intention to collaborate with their Rome Treaty partners. They declared that such collaboration did not contradict their desire to cooperate with non-Common Market countries, but pointed out that they could not accept any arrangement which would impede implementation of the Rome Treaty.

The search for a satisfactory arrangement between the European Economic Community and the other European countries narrowed down essentially to a question of the right relationship between the Six and the United Kingdom. Behind specific trade and economic problems, there remained the fundamental issue of the ultimate organization of Western Europe. On this question, uncertainty and disagreement marked the spectrum of opinion on both sides of the English Channel. Even ardent supporters of the Common Market were not sure whether the process of integration would end in a new federal state or in a form of international coordination stopping short of a real merger of sovereignty. In the absence of agreed objectives, tactical maneuvering rather than genuine negotiation characterized relations between the Six and the United Kingdom through most of 1959.

Within the Common Market, there were basic differences of view among the Six governments, and between some of them and the new EEC institutions, on the question of the Community's external relations. The Benelux countries, Germany, and Italy tended to see some merit in continued negotiations for a Europe-wide arrangement. The de Gaulle government strongly questioned the validity of the concept of a wider European association. The hardening of the French position generated some suspicion, particularly among the Dutch, that France might be seeking to replace the original concept of the Community with a new Franco-German alliance.

The Common Market's new executive Commission (see Chapter 3) exerted its own independent influence to urge that the Community be "outward-looking" and pursue liberal and constructive policies. The Commission supported closer coordination with the United States and Britain on such things as economic policy, aid to underdeveloped areas, and the further reduction of trade barriers. It denied the need, however, for a specific Europe-wide arrangement. Influential members of the Commission and leaders of the integration movement felt that the process of making the Community truly irreversible should be given overriding priority and that negotiations on a wider arrangement would hamper that process. They argued that it would be easier for the Community to pursue liberal external policies after it was more firmly established. Thus the Commission recommended that the Community accelerate the pace of integration, shorten the transitional stages provided by the Treaty of Rome, speed up the development of a common commercial policy, and strengthen the monetary solidarity of member countries.

EUROPE AT SIXES AND SEVENS

Despite internal strains, stresses, and disagreements, the Six rapidly accepted the Community as something more than a mere trading arrangement. They extended their cooperation to the fields of finance and monetary policy and foreign affairs by means of frequent meetings of the appropriate ministers of each country. Discussions of means for speeding the pace of integration and strengthening the Community institutionally were pressed.

In the meantime, seven "outside" countries—the United Kingdom, Norway, Denmark, Sweden, Austria, Switzerland, and Portugal—agreed to work together for some kind of a limited free-trade association as a countermeasure to the aims of the Six. The decision to go ahead with the formation of an alternative trading arrangement was reached in the summer of 1959. Meetings were held to iron out commercial differences and competitive problems; on November 20, 1959, the ministers of the Seven met in Stockholm to initial a convention which formalized the European Free Trade Association (EFTA). Official statements by the Seven governments emphasized that the EFTA was intended to facilitate a Europewide agreement. In effect, the action split Western Europe into two major trading blocs.

A prime reason for proceeding with the EFTA plan, apart from the impulse to retaliate, was to force the Six into an economic settlement on terms acceptable to British interests. As a unit, the Seven had a much greater degree of economic interdependence with the Six and gave greater urgency to the need for some accommodation. While only 14 percent of British exports went to the Community, half of Austria's exports, about 40 percent of Switzerland's, and about 30 percent of Denmark's and Sweden's exports went to the Six. As the leading member of the Seven, Britain substantially strengthened its bargaining power.

The EFTA convention, ratified by the Seven in the spring, entered into force on May 3, 1960. By this time, however, shifting currents of opinion buffeted British policy toward another direction. In the United Kingdom, a growing number of responsible groups, particularly in industry and the press, began to advocate that Britain join the Common Market. A number of proposals for bringing the Commonwealth into a broad new trading scheme were aired.

Several new factors had given the search for an accommodation between the Six and the other OEEC countries a new impulse: a United States decision to take a more active role in the effort to find a solution to Europe's division; agreement among the Six to accelerate the consolidation of the European Community to a point where it could not be undermined by economic adversity or political change; a growing fear, particularly among the Seven, that the continued drifting apart of the two trading groups would lead to intolerable political consequences; and the emergence of a fundamental reappraisal of British policy toward Europe.

In an effort to help break the stalemate in which the European problem had become fixed by the end of 1959, the United States took the initiative to call a Special Economic Conference of representatives from the Six, the Seven, the other OEEC countries, and Canada and the United States. Concerned about growing tensions which might weaken the NATO alliance, the United States was anxious to bring the two European groups together in a new cooperative effort which would transcend strictly European trade problems—that is, an effort to develop a more dynamic and better coordinated approach to the economic problems of the entire free world on the basis of a strengthened European-North American partnership.

A series of meetings—involving all the OEEC countries, the United States, Canada, and the Commission of the European Economic Community—were held in Paris in January 1960. There was no quick meeting of minds on substantive issues. The United Kingdom continued to argue for a trading arrangement embracing both the Six and the Seven. France sought to rule out such an arrangement once and for all in the conviction that a broader, looser organization would absorb and then dissolve the European Community. The United States hoped that trade barriers could be reduced globally rather than on a regional basis, but supported the Six in emphasizing the importance of consolidating the EEC.

The United States had become increasingly aware of the discriminatory effect of both European trading schemes on American trade, especially in light of its deteriorating balance-of-payments position. But the Common Market's political appeal—the goal of eventual union—offset its economic disadvantages in the eyes of American policymakers. The EFTA, lacking the objective of economic and political unity, received a cold American reception, even though it represented less of an obstacle to American exports than the European Community. Accordingly, the United States displayed little interest in joining the Seven to urge a renewal of negotiations on a wider area of free trade in Europe.

Despite important differences of views, the January meetings produced agreement on a number of procedural questions which prepared the way for future action to strengthen "Atlantic" economic cooperation. An American proposal to establish immediately a small committee of capital-export countries—the Development Assistance Group—to coordinate Western policies toward the underdeveloped countries was approved without great difficulty. General trade problems and ways of meeting any difficulties arising from the existence of the two European groups were to be considered by a special committee composed of the 18 OEEC members and the United States and Canada. It was also agreed that the 20 governments should consider the need for a "successor" organization to OEEC, and that a group of four experts—a Frenchman, an Englishman, an American, and a Greek—should prepare a report for this purpose. This decision did not imply that the OEEC had ceased to be a useful institution, but underscored a desire to re-establish relations between Europe and North America in a new context that would go beyond the postwar OEEC pattern.

Soon after the January economic meetings in Paris, the Commission of the European Community made public its proposals, submitted to the foreign ministers of the Six countries, for accelerating the Common Market. These were officially welcomed by the United States. The Commission outlined the various reasons that prompted its recommendations: (1) the improved economic situation in the Six countries, with a more satisfactory level of reserves; (2) better adjusted rates of exchange; (3) more stable financial situation; (4) less pronounced differences in economic and commercial policies than existed two years earlier when the Treaty of Rome was drafted. Moreover, formal acceleration of the customs union would simply conform to the rapid development of economic relations within the Community. Finally, the Commission reiterated its belief that "the sooner economic integration is achieved, the more surely will the commercial policy of the Community be dynamic, outward-looking, and liberal."

The Commission's proposals to speed up the customs union was received with mixed reactions within the Community. There was some concern, especially in Germany, that precipitate action might make more difficult an eventual accommodation with the Seven. The Council of Ministers of the Six supported acceleration in principle, but could not reach immediate agreement on details. The Seven, in the meantime, made it clear that they would regard acceleration as an unfriendly move and strongly resented indications of American support for the plans of the Six.

Prime Minister Macmillan took the occasion of a visit to Washington in March 1960 to warn the United States of the dangers he saw arising from the split in Europe. According to a widely quoted press report, he said that Britain would have no alternative but to lead another coalition against the Continental powers if the split continued. In addition to striking a parallel to British policy in the days of Napoleon, Mr. Macmillan was reported to have indicated that the adverse effects of the division might force the British to reimpose dollar import restrictions and further to reduce British troops in Germany. Certain aspects of the report were quickly denied by the Foreign Office. The Prime Minister himself, addressing the House of Commons shortly thereafter, insisted that his object had been not to weaken the Six, but to keep the economic split from developing into a more serious political division.

The Washington press report led to immediate and violent reaction on the Continent. It confirmed the belief of many European leaders that the United Kingdom was opposed to Continental unity. Rather than encourage caution and second thoughts, it strengthened support for acceleration of the Common Market both in Europe and in Washington. The Parliament of the Six was debating the acceleration proposals when news of the leak was received. The Assembly endorsed the Commission's plan quickly and almost without dissent, although earlier criticisms of the proposals had been numerous.

The Foreign Ministers of the Six, having already accepted the general principle of a speed-up, met in mid-May 1960 as the Council of Ministers of the Community to decide on the timing and other details of the acceleration plan. They agreed to reduce tariffs on intra-Community trade at least 40 percent—if conditions were favorable, 50 percent—by the end of 1961 and to advance the date for the first move toward the establishment of a common external tariff.

The Council reaffirmed its intention to accelerate as rapidly as possible, not simply the customs union, but also other aspects of the Treaty, particularly those dealing with such social questions as equal pay for men and women, occupational training, and freedom of movement of workers. In addition, a "declaration of intention" was adopted with regard to relations with third countries. This indicated the Community's determination to pursue a liberal policy, to take into account the principal interests of third countries, and to preserve, through negotiations, the traditional trade between the Community and the EFTA. The declaration made clear that the Community was not contemplating new negotiations on a comprehensive European agreement. The fact that the Community was a customs union had to be accepted as a starting point. Negotiations were viewed useful primarily in terms of mitigating the effects on trade of the existence of two European groups.

THE EMERGING BRIDGE

In subsequent months, the Seven reluctantly concluded that they had no alternative but to work with the Six on the solution of short-term difficulties affecting intra-European trade. At the same time, they now encouraged the Six to specify their requirements for a long-term settlement. This course had the effect of creating a growing impression that the Seven, and particularly Britain, were reconsidering their attitude toward the European Communities. In June 1960 the British Minister of State, Mr. John Profumo, indicated that the United Kingdom was willing to consider joining Euratom, the Coal and Steel Community, or both. This declaration was received with some suspicion on the Continent. The Six had been considering for some time the merging of the executive institutions of the three European Communities. There was some feeling that a British proposal to join only one or two of them represented simply another attempt to forestall the consolidation of the Six. The apparent change in Britain's position, however, gave rise to considerable speculation that the British government was preparing the way for a new and dramatic approach to the Community.

Events moved quickly in 1961 to bring both camps to a crucial cross-roads in their relations. The Seven arranged to accelerate their tariff reduction program to keep in step with the Six. Finland became an associate member of the EFTA and Greece of the EEC. As each bloc worked to improve its own sphere of operation, evidence of a new political will to agreement mounted. By summer, the EFTA countries had decided to seek acceptable terms for associating themselves individually with the EEC. A meeting of EFTA ministers in June acepted the principle of individual negotiation with the understanding that the unity of the Association would be maintained until all had reached satisfactory agreements. On July 31, 1961, Prime Minister Macmillan took the first step in opening formal negotiations by announcing that Britain would apply to the EEC for membership.

This dramatic and eventful decision marks the beginning of a new phase in Western Europe's evolving adjustment to the technological imperatives and political perils of the modern world. New mechanisms for channeling national rivalries and conflicts into nonviolent outlets are now being explored and tested. New institutions and procedures for consultation and action are being developed. They are helping to preserve the ability of independent states to influence their own destiny in a rapidly changing and increasingly complex world environment—and imperceptibly transforming the traditional meaning of sovereignty.

The economic and political entity emerging in Western Europe, as yet lacking an adequate nomenclature, will exert a decisive influence on the distribution of world power in the years to come (see Chapter 5). More importantly, its developing system of relations among states, resting at once on the independence and interdependence of nations, is laying a foundation for the construction of a new, and hopefully more viable, international order.

II   *European National Profiles*

I<small>N THE</small> light of present-day political, economic, and military realities, the unification of Western Europe would appear to an outsider so obviously necessary as to occasion little surprise. Europe as a whole—the smallest of the seven continents after Australia—is compact and crowded. The narrow terrain of the West European peninsula is densely populated and crisscrossed with an intricate network of commercial ties. Its major industrial complex, cramped in constricted space, is intersected by several national boundaries. Western Europe's coal and steel industry, for example, is heavily concentrated along a belt extending from the Ruhr in Germany through Luxembourg, Belgium, parts of the Netherlands, and Northern France. From a political and military point of view, long-range missile power adds an entirely new dimension to Western Europe's geographic significance: it is both a key strategic prize and a single tactical battlefield in the East-West conflict. The whole area can be viewed either as a trip-wire for signaling an attack from the East or as a beachhead for supporting a Western counterattack.

Nevertheless, despite all the factors working for Western Europe's integration, significant differences continue to stamp each country with its unique and vibrant identity. In view of the history and character of the individual nations involved, the imperfect co operation and unity already achieved border almost on the miraculous. Further progress will be largely dependent on the extent to which the process of regional integration is able to accommodate the aspirations, problems, needs, and rivalries of individual nations.

The forces now reshaping Western Europe, apart from those stemming from the requirements of the region as a whole, include such diverse factors as: the competition among Britain, France, and West Germany for position and influence as Europe's leading powers; the determination of weaker nations associated with the European Free Trade Association and the European Economic Community to safeguard their interests as active participants in Europe's affairs; the special needs of economically underdeveloped countries, such as Portugal, Spain, Greece, and Turkey; and the peculiar political difficulties facing Europe's neutrals—Finland, Sweden, Austria, and Switzerland.

Brief descriptions of these nations—large and small, at the center and at the periphery of European development—may help to indicate not only how much has been accomplished but also how much remains to be done.

UNITED KINGDOM

The world's chief power for a hundred years, Britain since World War I has faced the continuing task of adjusting to a rapidly declining power position. Perhaps its major challenge since World War II has been to maintain, in greatly altered form, beneficial ties with the more than 600 million people embraced by its former far-flung empire. Its great history and pride in democratic traditions and civil liberties have been a source of considerable strength in this painful transition. The sense of being set apart from the Continent as a vigorous and independent people remains strong in Britain even as this island-nation looks across the Channel for new means to assure its survival.

Located a short distance off the northwest coast of Europe, the United Kingdom is composed of four major geographic entities: England, Wales, Scotland, and Northern Ireland. Manufacturing and trade account for Britain's major occupations. Four-fifths of the United Kingdom's total population (some 52 million) lives in urban areas. The country imports all of its oil, cotton, rubber, sulphur, four-fifths of its wool, half of its food and iron ore, as well as amounts of paper, tobacco, and chemicals. Metals and metal-using industries contribute over 50 percent of its exports.

English dominance in the British Isles rests on a long history of political and religious conflict. In Wales (formally united with England since 1536), the spread of Calvinism during the 18th century played a large part in fostering Welsh nationalism. A struggle to disestablish the Church of England in Wales ended successfully in 1914. While Scotland and England were formally united in 1707, a nationalist movement, insisting on greater autonomy for Scotland, continues to retain some vigor. England officially incorporated Ireland following an Irish rebellion in 1798, but was never able to achieve permanent conquest. Northern Ireland, popularly called Ulster, became industrial and Protestant, while the rest remained rural and Catholic. Northern and Southern Ireland were divided in 1920, each acquiring its own parliament and government. When Ireland later became a republic, Northern Ireland elected to remain a part of the United Kingdom. (The Republic of Ireland refuses to accept the validity of this division.)

A vigorous tradition of imperial expansion helped shape Britain's view of its place among the nations of the world. England acquired its first colony (Newfoundland) in 1583, five years before the defeat of the Spanish Armada. Colonial and mercantile expansion during the 17th and 18th centuries, in competition with France and Holland, enabled the English merchant marine to gain commercial supremacy over the Dutch. By the end of the Seven Years' War (1763), Britain was mistress of the seas and had won control of North America and India. The American Revolution, a severe but temporary setback, was followed by British settlement of Australia and New Zealand as key elements in a spreading empire. Britain's role in the French revolutionary wars and in the defeat of Napoleon enhanced its position as a leading world power. During the 19th century, a new great period of imperial expansion, especially in Africa, brought the country unprecedented commercial and industrial prosperity.

The economic, political, and social instability that followed World War I led to efforts to strengthen British overseas interests in the face of changing conditions. Self-governing British dominions were granted the status of equality by the Statute of Westminster (1931), which created the concept of a British Commonwealth of Nations —a worldwide association of existing and former members of the British Empire. Far-sighted measures were instituted to train colonial wards toward eventual self-government. The liquidation of the empire following World War II advanced with startling rapidity as a score of colonies and protectorates achieved home rule or independence. Most of the new sovereignties chose to retain close economic and political ties with Britain as members of the Commonwealth. These ties, however, are being subjected to increasing strains, and their future is clouded in uncertainty.

The British system of government, an important influence on the political development of Commonwealth members (who acknowledge the Queen as head of the association), is a major element in Britain's sense of distinctiveness and separateness from the Continent. The United Kingdom is a parliamentary democracy in substance and a monarchy in form. The British take particular pride in the fact that their constitution has evolved through the centuries —melding Parliamentary statutes, common law, and traditional practices and precepts—and is constantly evolving. The British constitution has never been codified and, indeed, is largely unwritten. This vitality and adaptability to change account in large measure for the remarkable stability and resilience of British institutions.

The sovereign (the Queen), the executive government (with its civil service), and the two houses of Parliament (the House of Commons and the House of Lords) make up the central governmental structure. Technically, the Queen is the head of the executive and judiciary, an integral part of the legislature, commander-in-chief of all the armed forces, and temporal head of the Church of England. In practice, the Queen's legal powers have been transformed into instruments for carrying out the will of Parliament and the cabinet. She rules by approval of Parliament and can act, constitutionally, only on the advice of her ministers, who for over a century have been assigned directly more and more powers. As the British like to view it, the Queen reigns, but does not rule.

Parliament, the supreme legislative authority, includes representatives of all four territorial units of the United Kingdom, though Northern Ireland also has its own Parliament with power to legislate in certain spheres. Royal assent is required of all bills passed by Parliament and, for more than 200 years, has never been withheld. The House of Commons, elected by all British subjects over 20 years of age, is today far more powerful than the House of Lords, which consists of hereditary, spiritual, and life peers. The House of Lords can delay but not defeat measures passed by the House of Commons, where controversial bills are usually introduced.

The prime minister, nominally appointed by the sovereign, exercises executive power with a body of ministers. He and his aides must be members of Parliament. Traditionally, the prime minister is the leader of the majority party in Parliament. Since the House of Commons must approve the government's general policy and some of its specific measures, ministers are chosen mostly from this body, and normally belong to the prime minister's party. The leader of the official opposition is usually the leader of the chief minority party.

The party system of government in Britain dates from the latter part of the 17th century, when the final supremacy of Parliament was established. The ability of the Conservative party to adjust to new conditions and the rapid rise of the Labor party are perhaps the two outstanding phenomena of 20th-century British politics. In the 19th century, Conservatives and Liberals (successors to earlier Tory and Whig parties) were traditionally aligned against each other. After World War I, the Labor party rose to replace the Liberals as the official opposition. Entering Churchill's coalition government in World War II with the understanding that a broad social welfare program would be instituted after hostilities, the Laborites were elected to power in 1945. Basic industries were nationalized and a program of full employment through planned production was put into effect, along with various other social services in the fields of health, old-age care, and education.

Differences between the major parties narrowed considerably

thereafter. Conservatives, while calling for a halt to nationalization, indicated they would retain the changes already made and continue to promote the general welfare. Accepting much of Labor's social program, but promising to administer it more efficiently, the Conservatives were returned to power in 1951, in 1955, and again in 1959. Both parties are agreed on major issues and principles, differing mainly on the degree of state control in the economy and on the practical methods to be employed. Both affirm Britain's responsibility to exert a positive influence in international affairs.

Among the immediate problems facing the country as a whole are serious economic woes: inflation, balance of payments difficulties, and the threat of economic stagnation. Although possessing only about 2 percent of the world's population, the United Kingdom ranks second (after the United States) in world trade (contributing over 10 percent of the total). It serves as the central banker of the sterling area, which embraces one-fourth of the world's population (almost half the world's trade is conducted in sterling). Overseas investment, shipping, tourism, and various commercial and financial services contribute importantly to the national economy. With limited agricultural land and few natural resources (apart from coal and some low-grade iron ore), the country absorbs about a fifth of total world exports of primary products and accounts for about a fifth of total world exports of manufactures. It is one of the most highly industrialized nations in the world, with about 40 percent of the population concentrated in seven great metropolitan areas: London, Manchester, Glasgow, Birmingham, Leeds-Bradford, Liverpool, and Newcastle. For each agricultural worker, there are 11 workers in manufacturing, mining, and building. All of these factors underscore Britain's vulnerability to outside economic forces.

The country's present economic ills come at the heels of a period of outward and somewhat illusory prosperity. Despite a successful program of postwar recovery (involving rationing and price controls), wages rose faster than productivity. With the lifting of controls (except in certain agricultural products and in housing), the population's purchasing power exceeded the available supply of goods. Increased automation and adoption of mass production methods helped to raise industrial production, but the investment for modernization of plant and equipment on the whole was insufficient to sustain a continuous expansion of the economy. Britain's rate of economic growth became one of the lowest in Europe. The country found it increasingly difficult to compete with France and Germany, to earn enough overseas to pay for its heavy food and raw materials imports, and to build up the gold and foreign exchange reserves needed in present-day complex trade relationships.

The Macmillan government, in 1961, launched an austerity program and sought to enlist the cooperation of British labor and management in an effort to hold wages down and to work out jointly economic plans and policies to spur economic growth. A tripartite mechanism representing labor, industry, and government was established for the purpose of setting production goals and priorities, allocating essential resources, and charting basic export-import policies. The extent to which this effort will prove successful is an open question. It is clear, however, that the problems that inspire it are also a major factor impelling the United Kingdom toward closer ties with the Continent.

IRELAND (EIRE)

Some 800 years of bitterness and strife lie behind Ireland's present efforts to preserve and promote its independent development. Long centuries of British control of the island, coupled with persistent repression and misery, culminated in a series of uprisings and revolt movements at the end of the 19th century. Following considerable bloodshed during 1916-1921, the Anglo-Irish Treaty of 1922 established the Irish Free State as a British dominion. Irish aspirations for complete independence were not appeased. Adopting a new constitution in 1937, the 26 counties of Southern Ireland elected a president and officially changed the name of the country to Ireland (Eire in Gaelic). Ireland voted itself out of the British Commonwealth in 1948 and declared itself a republic in 1949. The desire to make the entire island one country remains the one great and sustaining political goal of the republic.

Despite its tenacious political zeal, the Republic of Ireland has relatively weak material resources with which to assert itself as a nation. Emigration, a traditional feature of Irish life, continues to drain the country of young men and women in search of economic opportunity. In recent years 40,000 persons have been leaving the country annually, mostly for the industrial cities of England. About three-fifths of Ireland's present inhabitants (under 3 million) live in rural areas. Successive governments since the 1920's have tried to encourage the development of diversified industries (by tariff protection and other means). Industrial production accounted for 25 percent of Ireland's national income in the mid-fifties; more than half of all industrial firms are still concentrated in Dublin and Cork.

In recent years, the government has promoted a comprehensive public investment program to counteract high rates of unemployment and emigration, concentrating on housing, hospitals, communications, roads, and electric power. Productive expenditure to increase national output, particularly of goods for the export market, has also been emphasized as a means to stimulate economic expansion. Various types of governmental assistance are used to encourage private enterprise and foreign investment in the country. Most of the country's trade is conducted with Great Britain and Northern Ireland (about 80 percent of the republic's exports go to the United Kingdom), but trade relations are also being developed with the United States, West Germany, India, the Netherlands, Belgium-Luxembourg, France, Canada, Australia, and other countries.

Economic hardships notwithstanding, the Republic of Ireland faces the outside world with pride in its culture and independence and with a stubborn determination to build up its economic and national strength. Ireland's application to enter the Common Market as a full member, revealing a readiness to accept the risks as well as the opportunities of full-scale European competition, provides a measure of the country's confidence in its future.

ICELAND

The westernmost European country, Iceland (Lydveldid Island) boasts a distinguished ancient heritage, although it has been a completely independent republic only since 1944. Only about 1 percent of its total population (around 180,000) is foreign-born, making for a high degree of cultural unity. The language of the country, Icelandic, has changed so little through the span of time that Icelanders are still able to read great 13th-century sagas without special study.

For centuries a dominion of Denmark, Iceland was declared a free and independent state in 1918; the Danish king, however, continued to function as king of Iceland. Cut off from Denmark in World War II, the country established diplomatic relations with the United Kingdom and the United States and accepted the protection of British and American forces. A referendum ended the union with the king of Denmark in 1944.

Iceland's strategic location and dependence on trade and fishing combine to press the demands of the outside world on this otherwise isolated island. Internal issues and controversy revolve around the country's role in NATO, the presence of American military installations, problems of economic development, and control of adequate fishing grounds (involving an extension of territorial waters). Although an original member of NATO, Iceland has no military establishment of its own. It does maintain armed vessels and planes for "fishery protection." At NATO meetings, Icelandic delegates attend the political but not the military sessions.

Most of Iceland's foreign exchange earnings come from fish exports. Since 1953, United States defense expenditures on coastal radar stations and on a NATO airfield have provided about 20 percent of the country's total foreign exchange receipts. With most of the land unsuitable for cultivation and with a short growing season, crop raising plays a very small role in the economy. Except for fish, meat, eggs, and dairy products, the country must import almost all of its requirements. Indigenous industry, heavily dependent on imported raw and semimanufactured materials, is small-scale and designed to meet local needs. Nevertheless, a high rate of capital investment (in housing, agriculture, communications, transportation, and fisheries) is generating a rapid development of the economy.

Despite Iceland's growing involvement in the affairs and frictions of the Atlantic Alliance, the nation continues to retain much of its traditional insular character.

DENMARK

Commanding the sea approaches to the Soviet Union through the Baltic, the Kingdom of Denmark (consisting of Denmark proper, the Faroe Islands, and Greenland) must accommodate many outside influences to preserve its security and prosperity. It is firmly tied to the rest of Western Europe as a member of NATO, but is also hopeful of maintaining amicable relations with Russia. The United States is permitted to have a vital military base on Greenland but not on Danish home soil. Neutralist tendencies and latent pacifism are pronounced in the country, yet the government has firmly resisted Soviet threats directed at frightening Denmark out of NATO.

Preferring to concentrate on internal affairs, the Danes nevertheless recognize that their safety is greatly influenced by trends and developments abroad over which they have little or no control. Once enjoying hegemony over Sweden and Norway (the latter remained united with Denmark until 1814), Denmark directed its energies at the end of the 19th century toward internal reforms and development. Specialization in dairy production and other economic changes transformed the country from a nation of poor peasantry to one of prosperous smallholders. While a neutral in World War I the country found itself at the mercy of Germany in World War II. The lesson of Nazi occupation in 1940 has not been forgotten since.

Though reluctant to become actively involved in the affairs and quarrels of larger powers, Denmark since the war has displayed a vigorous loyalty to its international commitments. Always a prominent maritime nation, it has also shown great resourcefulness in meeting difficult international economic competition. Despite relatively high living standards and purchasing power, the Danish domestic market is limited by a small population (about 4.5 million). Most important industries need foreign markets in order to expand. Active in shipbuilding and in large-scale foreign construction, the country has important investments abroad and depends considerably on shipping operating entirely in foreign waters.

With limited natural resources, Denmark must import raw materials, feeds, fertilizers, and fuels. Paying for these imports, dairy products and meats make up the bulk of Danish exports. In recent years, the traditional high-quality agricultural exports have been supplemented by a large expansion in the exportation of diverse manufactured goods. In fact, Danish manufacturing since World War II has gained so rapidly that it now contributes more to the national income than does agriculture. In producing for world markets, Danish manufacturers tend to concentrate on specialized quality products. Danish imports generally exceed exports, however, and the country has some difficulty in accumulating adequate foreign exchange reserves. Deficiencies in recent years have been held to reasonable proportions as a result of earnings from tourism, various services, and the Danish merchant fleet. Nevertheless, this problem has helped to produce some internal political pressure to limit Danish financial support to international organizations.

With a long-entrenched middle-of-the-road socialist government, Denmark (a constitutional monarchy) has the distinction of being one of the first countries in the world to establish effective social welfare services. Public relief is available to any incapacitated person living in the country. Unemployment insurance is widespread but voluntary. Insurance against work accidents has been in force since 1898. The concern with social welfare and health insurance has bound Denmark with other Scandinavian countries in a cooperative effort to establish uniform legislation in these fields.

Since a large part of its farm produce is exported to Continental countries, Denmark has welcomed the opportunity to link itself with the Common Market without prejudicing its interests or commitments as a member of the European Free Trade Association (See Chapter 4).

NORWAY

Part of Denmark until 1814 and linked with Sweden until 1905, Norway shares many of the characteristics of its Scandinavian neighbors: a constitutional monarchy; a deep emotional kinship with the West filtered by strong neutralist sentiment; pioneering efforts in the field of social welfare (public assistance has been available in the country since 1845); a highly homogenous people with no significant minority groups; a heavy dependence on foreign trade; and a vigorous sense of independence (courageously expressed in a magnificent resistance movement during World War II). A neutral during World War I, Norway was invaded by Nazi Germany in 1940, after 125 years of undisturbed peace. After the war, abandoning its former neutrality, the country accepted Marshall Plan aid and joined NATO.

Endowed with a long coastline and vast forests, Norway traditionally has been a fishing and lumbering country. Foreign trade, a critical factor in the economy, normally contributes almost half of the country's gross national product. Lacking a large domestic market (population: 3.6 million), Norway is quick to feel the effects of fluctuations in world prices and shipping rates and of recessions in the United States or the United Kingdom. About half the total value of foreign payments comes from shipping. Fishing (including whaling), forestry (including pulp and paper), and mining and electrochemical industries provide the largest part of Norwegian exports. Base metals are particularly important as a principal export. While mineral deposits are not extensive, considerable quantities of copper and iron pyrites and iron ore are mined.

Most of Norway's domestic food requirements are met by local agriculture, employing 18 percent of the labor force and accounting for about 6 percent of the country's national income. The country imports, however, significant amounts of tropical fruits, vegetables, coffee, tea, cocoa, spices, and cereals. The economic sector undergoing the most intensive development is industry. Manufacturing has grown rapidly since World War I and contributes about 30 percent of the gross national product. Abundant low-cost hydroelectric power is being used to diversify industrial products, based largely on the processing of domestic wood, fish, and metal ores. Handicrafts, supported by low-interest government loans, are expanding. The development of new regional industries, particularly in areas with substantial unemployment, is being pushed with a governmental tax concession and loan campaign.

Politically, Norway has enjoyed a stable Labor-dominated government since 1935. Executive power, constitutionally vested in the king, is exercised through a cabinet (the Council of State), theoretically chosen by the king but actually selected by the parliament (Storting). The parliament has served as the dominant governing authority in Norway since 1864. It controls finances and has the power to override the king's veto. The economic depression in the 1930's resulted in the establishment of a Labor government which has maintained its power ever since. During World War II, the country's main political parties (ranging from Conservatives to Liberals) formed a national cabinet-in-exile. This political truce continued after the war, despite some sharpening of differences between right and left. Major internal controversies in recent years have centered on internal issues—domestic price controls and budget provisions—rather than on foreign policy.

Like Denmark, however, Norway has shown great relief that a way has been opened for bridging the differences between the European Free Trade Association and the Common Market (see Chapter 5). Norwegian leaders look forward to the possibilities of full membership in the European Economic Community as a means of participating more actively in Europe's development.

SWEDEN

Fourth in size among the countries of Europe, the Kingdon of Sweden is considered by some the most nationalistic Scandinavian country. National defense, freedom from entangling alliances, and economic growth are the major issues of national concern. Following a neutralist foreign policy, the country is determined not to get embroiled in a war. While refusing to join NATO, it did become a member of the United Nations in 1946 and has placed some of its military forces under UN command.

Swedes like to view their "neutralism" not as an escape from contemporary realities but as a realistic affirmation of their national purpose. They are ready to repulse any aggression with vigor. With about 25 percent of their national budget allocated for defense, they possess one of the best armies and air forces on the Continent. Sweden's civil defense measures, perhaps the most advanced in Europe, include the world's most elaborate underground air raid shelters. Its neutralist posture gives it some flexibility in dealing with other nations. Its sympathies, however, are unequivocally with the West, which relies on Sweden as a useful channel for informal contacts and airing of view with hostile or neutral political interests.

Governed under the oldest written constitution in force in Europe (dating from 1809), Sweden has gained the reputation of being one of the world's most progressive countries. The Social Democratic Labor party, in power almost uninterruptedly since 1932, has pushed various huge social welfare programs. Postwar economic expansion lasted until about 1953, when inflation became a serious and continuing problem. Although a number of Swedish industries are nationalized, private business still accounts for 93 percent of the value of Sweden's industrial output.

Predominantly agricultural in the 19th century, Sweden now has only about 15 percent of its approximately 7 million people earning a living in agriculture. Production per man-hour in Swedish agriculture has increased by 90 percent since the 1940's, permitting the country to export from 8 to 10 percent of its agricultural output (although a large amount of foodstuffs is also imported).

Swedish industry has expanded rapidly as a supplier of quality goods and specialized products—ball bearings, high-grade steel, machine tools, and glassware. Forests, iron ore, and water power are the basic resources for industrial development. The economy's distinctive features include: a spread of factories to rural districts; a close contact between trade, industry, and finance; and increased application of automation and control devices in industrial plants. One-half of all industrial salaried employees and one-third of all industrial workers are employed by the engineering industry, which accounts for about 35 percent of total industrial production. The emphasis in industry since World War II has been on the manufacture of export items.

Sweden's principal exports include: paper, electrical and other machinery, iron ore, wood and its products, high-grade steels, and engineering products. Leading imports consist of minerals, foodstuffs, machinery, and base metals. West Germany and the United Kingdom rank high among the biggest suppliers of Swedish imports and the biggest purchasers of Swedish products. Other major trade partners include: the United States, Norway, the Netherlands, Denmark, France, Belgium-Luxembourg, Italy, and Brazil.

As a neutral, Sweden has been reluctant to endorse the Common Market movement, principally because of its political aims. For a time, the Swedes bitterly resented American hostility toward the formation of a free-trade area as an alternative to the European Economic Community. They have come to accept the Common Market, however, as the unavoidable reality that will dominate Europe's future. Sweden is now prepared to negotiate for some kind of economic association with the European Economic Community and, joined by Austria and Switzerland, can be expected to press for arrangements that will take into account the special requirements of political neutrality.

FINLAND

Occupying one of the "neuralgic" corners of the Cold War, Finland finds itself in the painful position of trying to accommodate Soviet interests while seeking to maintain close economic and cultural ties with other Scandinavian democracies and with the West generally. Vulnerable to subtle but powerful Russian influence and control, the country serves as a channel for transmitting Soviet pressure throughout Scandinavia. Recent Soviet demands on Finland appear to have been partly designed to persuade Sweden, Norway, and Denmark to withdraw from the Western orbit into a Northern European neutral belt.

Finland was annexed by Russia in 1809, after centuries of Swedish rule, and achieved independence in 1917. Two years later the country became a democratic parliamentary republic. It scored noteworthy economic and social advances during the interwar period. Its neutral pro-Scandinavianism in the 1930's, however, failed to protect its security. Unavoidably entangled in the worsening relations between the great powers, the country fought two heroic wars with the Soviet Union (1939-1940 and 1941-1944). The country was obliged to cede territory and to pay reparations to the USSR. Present relations with the Soviet Union are governed by a Treaty of Friendship and Mutual Assistance signed in 1948. The preamble of this treaty recognizes "Finland's desire to remain out of the conflicting interests of the Great Powers."

Topography and culture combine to make this a particularly unique country. With one-third of its total length above the Arctic Circle, it has land border with Sweden, Norway, and the USSR. A severely indented coastline and thousands of small islands etch its southern and western coastal plain. The majority of the country's 55,000 lakes are located in central Finland, an extensive lake plateau. North Finland consists of densely forested upland. Internal lakes and canals, with a floatable length of 26,500 miles, provide important natural waterways. Handicapped by relatively poor soil, severe northern climate, and a lack of coal and other mineral resources, the land sustains a population of 4.4. million.

Although about 90 percent of the people speak Finnish (related to Estonian and, more remotely, to Hungarian), Swedish is recognized as the country's second legal language. Migrating to Finland by way of the Baltic regions during the first centuries after Christ, the Finns have maintained much of their ethnic distinctiveness. More than six centuries of attachment to the Swedish realm, however, deeply influenced the development of Finnish economic life, social order, and political institutions and processes. These were marked by a gradual growth of constitutionalism and self-government. When annexed by Tsarist Russia, Finland enjoyed a privileged autonomous status (which was revoked, however, with the growth of a Finnish nationalist movement toward the end of the 19th century).

While suffering an estimated 100 famine years from the 14th through the 19th centuries, the Finns today have surmounted their environmental handicaps to build a surprisingly productive and diversified economy. A number of factors have made the achievement of a fairly substantial standard of living possible: a disposition toward hard work, frugality, and ingenuity; unrivaled supplies of forests (Finland's "green gold"); and substantial water-power resources ("white gold"). Timber, wood products, and paper- and pulp-producing industries are highly developed and provide the overwhelming proportion of the country's exports.

Only about 8 percent of Finnish land is arable, and a relatively small proportion is under cultivation. Recent improvements in agriculture have emphasized specialization in dairying and cattle breeding. Milk production exceeds domestic needs (permitting the export of butter and cheese), but the country is only 40 percent self-sufficient in cereals. As in all Scandinavian countries, fishing provides an important source of food.

The Finnish economy, very sensitive to changes at the international level, is dependent on foreign sources for a large portion of its raw materials, fuels, and machinery. Its principal trade partners include: the United Kingdom, the USSR, West Germany, Sweden, France, the United States, the Netherlands, and Belgium-Luxembourg. Trade has been steadily increasing with the USSR and declining with Germany and the United Kingdom, a change from the prewar pattern. Unemployment and inflation constitute major internal problems.

Overshadowing Finland's vigorous struggle to maintain its economic viability is the constant need to meet internal and external pressures aimed at transforming the republic into a "people's democracy" on the Soviet pattern. For the present, however, its semi-independent status on the fringe of the Soviet empire appears both adequate and useful from the viewpoint of Soviet interests. Finland won Soviet permission to join the European Free Trade Association as an associate member (see Chapter 4) in part because the Russian leaders hoped this might help to counter or deflect the Common Market's growing momentum. The Finns would like to work out some sort of economic link with the European Economic Community. But with less freedom to maneuver than enjoyed by the Austrians, they realize this may take a long time in the face of protracted Soviet opposition.

PORTUGAL

Modern Portugal, as though matching the sharp topographic contrasts of the Iberian Peninsula, presents a strikingly anachronistic image as a participant in current world affairs. Staunchly anticommunist, it supported the Allies during World War II, became one of the 12 original signatories to NATO, and joined the United Nations in 1955. A corporate republic, it is ruled by a benevolent dictatorship which, though lacking the ruthlessness of a totalitarian system, seeks to preserve the elaborate structure of a highly centralized and authoritarian political, economic, and social system. Portugal proper has hardly been touched by the great changes and upheavals that have swept Europe in the past three decades. Its chief internal problem is poverty (its per capita income of $230 per year is one of the lowest in Europe).

The country thus far has managed to hold on to many of the fruits of early maritime exploration and is now the largest colonial empire in the world. Although Brazil, the wealthiest of Portuguese overseas territories, declared its independence in 1822 and became a republic in 1889, vast African and Asian territories were knitted into the Portuguese national structure. Determined to resist convulsive anti-colonial movements, Portugal renamed itself an "Afro-European" power in 1951 and changed the status of its overseas possessions, under law, into integral provinces of the metropolitan country. Its two largest overseas provinces (Angola and Mozambique) have a combined area of about 783,600 square miles.

Portugal's mounting colonial difficulties are a source of great strain within the Western alliance, particularly in view of American support of the "legitimate" aspirations of underdeveloped and newly emerging countries. Other European nations, though not necessarily in sympathy with Portugal's internal or colonial administration, are concerned with the implications that American policies and attitudes may have for their own substantial overseas interests. Portugal itself has sought to use the condemnation of its colonial policies in the United Nations and elsewhere to rally internal support around its flag and present regime. The country is not free of internal political discontent, though opposition forces thus far have been divided and without organized focus.

While upholding the sanctity of private property, the government supervises, controls, and regulates the economic life of the country through a system of corporations, syndicates, and guilds. Employers, workers, farmers, rural laborers, fishermen, and professional people are all organized in some form of association representing the same economic, social, or professional activity. Slowdowns, lockouts, strikes, and similar expressions of grievances are prohibited. Agriculture, the mainstay of the economy, employs the largest segment of the population (50 percent of the labor force). Small and "dwarf-sized" farms dot the central and northern sections of the country; large estates with plentiful labor are found mostly in the southern section. In most areas, mechanization is poorly developed.

Industry received some stimulus by Marshall Plan aid after World War II and is mainly light (a shortage of electric power has hampered the development of heavy industry). Leading Portuguese industries include: textiles, glass, pottery, cement, paper, rubber and chemicals, cork products, and food industries (mainly canned fish). Constant population increases (present population: between 8 and 9 million) have provided a large labor force at low wage levels, but industrial productivity is generally low.

Importing foodstuffs, raw materials, fuels, machinery and equipment, and consumer goods, Portugal exports principally raw and manufactured cork (most of it bought by the United States), wines, cotton textiles, canned fish, naval stores, and minerals. Its most important trade partner is the United Kingdom (which has an unbroken political alliance with Portugal dating from 1386). Portugal's balance-of-payments figures have regularly shown a net loss in foreign trade. This deficit, however, has been more than balanced by a substantial income derived from the overseas provinces. Forced labor has been a basic element in the economy of colonial possessions, and the extent to which Portugal will be able to depend on its overseas income in the future in problematical.

Portugal's failure to receive strong backing from its allies for its overseas policies has weakened the country's loyalty to the European Free Trade Association and, in particular, to the United Kingdom. The need for political support—as much as the need for economic aid—has encouraged Portugal to seek firmer ties with the Common Market countries on the Continent.

SPAIN

The Spanish State—technically a monarchy with the throne vacant—presents a combination of economic weakness and geographic strength. With a per capita income of $265 a year, its standard of living, after Portugal, is the lowest in Western Europe. Spain received no Marshall Plan aid after World War II and is still trying to recover from the wounds of its traumatic Civil War. It has been kept out of NATO, not because of its dictatorship, but because the present regime owes its power to Nazi-Fascist support in the 1930's. Nevertheless, sheltered by the Pyrenees, enjoying a geographically strong position at the entrance to the Mediterranean, and within medium-bomber range of the Soviet Union, the country occupies a strategically important location.

With the objective of obtaining air and naval bases, the United States established a quasi-alliance with Spain in 1953, bringing it into the Western defense system at the cost of substantial economic aid. American support helped get Spain admitted to the United Nations in 1955 and the Organization for European Economic Cooperation (OEEC) in 1959. The country, however, remains, in large measure, politically isolated from the rest of Western Europe. Ostracized, Spain also must contend with Italian and British rival interests in the Mediterranean, the Arab world, and over Gibraltar. American bases in Spain are losing some of their value in terms of defense against a Soviet attack as a result of rapid ballistic-missile development. Their importance as an approach to North Africa, on the other hand, may be increasing. This advantage, however, is offset by the fact that Spain as presently ruled remains a political liability to the United States from the point of view of American interests in many of the countries of Europe.

A chief of state (caudillo) and a council of ministers, appointed by the chief of state, constitute the central government. The Cortes is the legislative organ of the state but subject to the absolute veto of the caudillo. Most of the 577 members of the Cortes are elected for three-year terms to represent all sectors of national life. The chief of state, however, appoints the president, two vice presidents, four secretaries, and some 50 members of the Cortes. The only sanctioned political party is the Falange. Head of the Falange party, General Francisco Franco Bahamonde has served as chief of state since 1939 and was "granted" life tenure in this position in 1947. Under a law promulgated at that time, a regency council is supposed to enthrone a king of his choice as his successor. If a successor is not named before the caudillo's death, the regency council is to present the name of a king or regent to the Cortes.

The state reserves to itself the right to participate in the management of all economic activities. Through a National Institute of Industry, the government has made some effort to stimulate industrialization. Production, however, still does not meet the requirements of the domestic market. Industrial development has been retarded by shortages of essential resources—steel, modern machinery, high-grade coal, electric power, and transportation facilities—and by restrictive legislation against foreign capital. State monopolies, controlled by a close friend of General Franco, include: mining enterprises, oil refineries, steel and chemical plants, ship-building yards, artificial fiber factories, tobacco and cigarettes, and the bulk of petroleum products.

Essentially an agricultural country, Spain has over 50 percent of its total labor force engaged in farming. Farm holdings vary greatly in size, type of ownership, and operating procedures. Small farms with tenant farmers operating on long-term leases are typical in the north. Large estates and short-term tenancy contracts are more prevalent in the south. The more important agricultural products include: cereals (particularly wheat), oranges, rice, olives, grapes, nuts, cotton, and tobacco.

The country's foreign trade is characterized by the export of agricultural products and minerals and the import of machinery and industrial materials. The United States is Spain's most important supplier of imports, whereas the United Kingdom serves as its principal market for exports. The economy as a whole, in many areas, is still at a standstill. Recovery from the Civil War, which came at the heels of the depression of the 1930's, has been slow. The position of the economy showed some improvement, however, after American loans (both in cash and food surpluses) in the 1950's eased the country's economic isolation.

The weakness of the Spanish economy seriously limits the progress that Spain can make in the direction of economic integration with Western Europe. Barring any internal upheaval, the process of forming closer ties with other European nations can be expected to be slow and gradual. Internal discontent, though lacking unity and organizational power, is nevertheless growing in intensity. Opposition forces embrace a wide spectrum of political and social beliefs, and include anarchists, socialists, communists, monarchists, and Basque and Catalan nationalist groups.

ITALY

With a history extending over 2,500 years, the Italian nation, except for Greece, is the oldest in Europe. Yet even today, a large part of the population has a stronger sense of allegiance to family, city, and regional ties than to the country as a whole. Suffering a succession of crises since World War II, Italy has sought to bury the bitter memories of Fascism while trying to strengthen its economic and political foundations. With over 50 percent of its labor force in industry, Italy has shown considerable economic progress, especially in the past several years. Despite advances, however, the country remains desperately poor. Unemployment—in the 2 million range in the mid-1950's—has been reduced but is still a large problem. The striking contrasts between Italy's industrial north and feudal south dramatize the sharp disparity that exists between rich and poor. Large areas of southern Italy are still untouched by economic development. As one observer put it: "Below Naples, Italy is Africa."

Coupled with poverty is the difficult problem of maintaining political stability. No single party is strong enough to command a clear majority. Each tends to be authoritarian and dogmatic in insisting on the "rightness" of its own views and programs. As a result, the republic (established by plebiscite in 1946) has had to contend with a series of short-lived coalition governments. Communists and socialists, a potent political force when working in partnership, together command the votes of about 40 percent of the electorate. The tensions and discontents generated by modernization provide large opportunities for communist agitation and subversion. The Christian Democratic party, at the center of the political spectrum, has thus far maintained itself in power despite factional strife, but must face persistent pressures seeking to sever Italy's political and military ties with the rest of Western Europe, particularly in NATO.

A principal objective of current governmental policy is to correct the imbalance of the Italian economy. Large-scale investments in industry, public works, building, and agriculture have been supported by domestic and foreign financial resources. A Southern Fund, established in 1950, has borrowed substantial sums from European and international institutions for the rehabilitation and development of southern Italy. Government participation in several sectors of the economy (medium and heavy industry, insurance, and credit) is strong. Italy's internal development task may absorb the energies of more than a decade and greatly limit the country's ability to contribute to the development of foreign areas, whether through European or international institutions.

Both industry and farming are characterized by small enterprises. Over half of all Italian farmers work on land averaging 1.2 acres or less. The bulk of industrial workers (some 75 percent) are found in establishments employing not more than two workers. Italian heavy industry, on the other hand, is characterized by relatively large enterprises. It has scored a spectacular revival since World War II, establishing world-wide reputation in new industrial products (such as sewing machines, optics, and chemicals).

Italian industry is handicapped by a lack of domestic raw materials and fuels. Industrial resources (with the exception of hydroelectric power and natural gas) are inadequate to support the country's development plans. Almost all of the petroleum, cotton, copper, and phosphate rock, about 90 percent of its coal, and a major part of its wool, cellulose, and iron must be imported. Similarly, a scarcity of good soils, water available for irrigation, and capital limit Italian agricultural development. Sizable quantities of wheat must be imported even though Italy is a cereal-producing country. The supply of domestic wheat and the import of foreign wheat are subject to government controls.

Mechanization, crop rotation, and seed improvement have led to a rise in agricultural production in recent years. A varied climate and topography make the country well suited for raising vegetables and fruits (both early and late crops), and these remain the country's principal agricultural exports. New markets for certain crops (such as citrus and other fruits) are being developed. Wheat, corn, oats, barley, and rye are among the country's leading crops. Major industrial crops include olive oil, hemp, flax, and tobacco. In many districts, potatoes and rice are also important. Grapes are grown in large quantities, but used chiefly in the production of domestic wines.

Italy's main trade partners include: the United States, West Germany, the United Kingdom, Switzerland, France, and Austria. The shortage of energy resources, however, makes the country vulnerable to trade overtures by the Soviet bloc. Soviet petroleum, in particular, has successfully penetrated the Italian market in recent years. A substantial increase in this penetration, if permitted to develop into a dependence on Soviet oil, could have an adverse effect on Italy's ties with the rest of Western Europe.

Although endowed with a great and illustrious heritage, the nation today finds almost all of its energies absorbed in current economic, social, and political problems. Italy's tremendous contributions to the worlds of government and law, art and letters, religion, and philosophy inspire pride but no longer serve as guideposts for the future. Since the downfall of Benito Mussolini's regime during World War II, the people have more or less turned their backs on synthetic efforts to revive the glories of their past and look on their ancient monuments primarily as a source of increasingly important tourist income.

Despite many difficulties, Italy's economy has made large strides since the country joined the Common Market. Its gross national product increased 8.8 percent in 1960 over 1959 and 9.2 percent in 1961 over the previous year. Unemployment no longer appears as an incurable disease. Indeed, Italian industry is now held back by an emerging shortage of skilled labor. Its great progress is helping to weld Italy to the Common Market as one of its most vigorous and enthusiastic members.

GREECE

Once a fountainhead of Western civilization, the Kingdom of Greece today finds itself in the throes of economic and political discontent. It shares with Italy the problems of large-scale unemployment and underemployment. As in Scandinavia, neutralist appeals come in conflict with the country's official allegiance to the Western defense structure, including NATO. Volatile and proud, the people are determined to preserve their integrity as a nation, but conscious of their weakness when confronting the outside world. Direct and indirect communist pressure has been a constant problem since World War II. Conflict with Britain and Turkey over Cyprus (which is about 80 percent Greek) had been a source of strain within NATO until the island was granted independence in 1959.

Indeed, foreign rivalries and interests have played a large part in the shaping of modern Greece. The country became a Turkish province when Constantinople fell to the Turks in 1453 and regained its independence only in the 19th century. The cause of Greek revolutionists, romanticized by the English poet Byron, won sympathy throughout Europe. In 1832, motivated by practical political and economic considerations, France, England, and Russia joined to guarantee Greek independence. A Bavarian prince was established as King Otto but he was forced to abandon the throne after an insurrection in 1862. England then had Prince William of Denmark succeed to the kingship as George I, who gave Greece a new constitution and its first parliamentary government. Military leaders assumed control of the country after World War I. A plebescite in 1924 transformed the country into a republic, though a military dictatorship took over again in the mid-1930's. The Axis occupation of World War II, an era of oppression and starvation, lasted until 1944. Struggles for power among various Greek resistance groups erupted into a violent civil war in which communists tried to seize control of the country. George II was restored to the throne by a plebiscite in 1946 (succeeded by Paul I, his brother, the following year). With American aid, communist efforts at takeover were blocked, and the civil war was brought to a close in 1949. In an effort to guarantee its security, Greece joined NATO in 1951 and also signed a defensive alliance with Yugoslavia and Turkey in 1953.

Although over 30 parties are active in the country's political life today, individual leaders are more important than party platforms. Most of the parties are agreed on a number of general objectives: improvements in social security programs, higher salaries and pensions, reforms in governmental administration, monetary stability, and broad economic progress. The issues which arouse the most controversy concern such matters as subservience to foreign powers in external affairs, support of NATO bases, and protection of political liberties.

The Greek economy is based on agriculture, although manufacturing is growing in importance as an income earner. The country is self-sufficient in wheat, rice, and potatoes, but must still meet many of its food needs through imports. In an effort to increase farm production, the government has pressed programs of land reclamation, more intensive cultivation, irrigation, and the use of scientific farming methods. Various measures are adopted to encourage farm prosperity, including the exemption of agricultural income from most taxes and also direct subsidies. The principal agricultural products are tobacco (providing about 45 percent of export earnings), cereals, grapes, olives, cotton, potatoes, truck garden vegetables, citrus fruits, and dried fruits.

Greek industry—dependent on imports for raw materials, machinery, and fuel—is limited by heavy taxation and social insurance charges, a shortage of low-cost credit, and the absence of a capital market. Industrial production has not risen far beyond the prewar level. The chief industries are textiles, chemicals, foodstuffs, and beverages. A vigorous program of electrification is being pushed as the keystone of future economic progress. The government hopes that adequate low-priced electric power will encourage industries, boost agricultural production, provide savings of foreign exchange, and raise the people's general standard of living.

Owing to its great dependence on imports for essential resources, Greece has a chronic deficit in its balance of payments. As in the case of Italy, tourism and the remittances of Greek citizens who emigrate to foreign countries are a substantial aid to the balance of payments. West Germany, the United States, the United Kingdom, Italy, France, and Austria are among the country's main trade partners.

The treaty of association between Greece and the Common Market (see Chapter 4) presents the country with one of the largest challenges in its economic history. It calls for the gradual "Europeanization" of the Greek economy—a process expected to span a period of over twenty years.

TURKEY

Geographically and culturally, Turkey serves as a bridge between Europe and Asia. Lying athwart the important Black Sea straits system (the Dardanelles, the Sea of Marmara, and the Bosporus), the country borders Bulgaria and Greece to the west, Iraq and Syria to the south, and the USSR and Iran to the east. Its population (98.0 percent Muslim) has been subjected to intensive Westernization since the end of World War I. Firmly committed to the web of Western alliances, Turkey is a member of both the North Atlantic Treaty Organization (NATO) and the Central Treaty Organization (CENTO), formed to stem the communist tide in the Middle East. Its history has left it with a strong traditional fear and hatred of Russia. At the same time, however, an undertow of anti-Americanism has grown in strength in recent years. Lacking experience in democracy, Turkey is still searching for ways to grapple effectively with serious political, economic, and administrative problems.

Although neutral during most of World War II, Turkey was pro-Allied and declared war on the Axis early in 1945. A charter member of the United Nations, it received large-scale American military and economic assistance to counter mounting Soviet pressure in 1947. Continuing American aid encouraged intensive efforts to accelerate the nation's economic development. The government reoriented its economic policy from one of state capitalism (pursued during the 1930's) to a freer economic regime. Various measures were taken to develop private enterprise and to attract private foreign enterprise. Mixed private-public ventures (such as the Turkish Airways Corporation) became common. Government ownership and operation remained important in many economic fields, but the expansion of state enterprise was linked more closely to the needs of private enterprise.

The country derives about half of its national income directly from agriculture. Most of the arable land is cultivated, with an average holding of from 10 to 15 acres. Although modern machinery has been introduced in many areas, agricultural methods tend to be primitive. Much of the land is able to sustain little more than a subsistence standard of living. Cereals take up about 90 percent of the cultivated area. Crops of commercial importance include world-famous tobacco, cotton, fruits, nuts, and olives. Inefficient land use, an alarming erosion rate, droughts, and failure to adopt modern farming methods are among the major agricultural problems facing the country today.

The mechanization of agriculture, though gradual, has contributed to significant population shifts from rural to urban areas. These shifts have necessitated a high rate of investment (between 11 and 15 percent of the gross national product) in urban and industrial development. Over-all industrial production has doubled since the end of World War II. Hundreds of small machine shops account for much of the production of machines, consumer goods, and tools. Sugar, beverages, tobacco products, textiles, paper, petroleum, iron and steel, cement, and chemicals are among the major industrial enterprises. Few manufactured goods are exported.

About 90 percent of all Turkish exports consist of agricultural products (principally tobacco, fruits, and nuts), although the country is also a net importer of foodstuffs (except in good crop years). Machinery and transport equipment, petroleum and products, wheat, and chemicals are among the main imports. The country trades heavily both with Western and Iron Curtain economies. In trying to make its own economy competitive, however, Turkey has become heavily indebted to Western creditors. While loans and credits have enabled it to purchase vital machinery for both agriculture and industry, the total foreign debt equals about one-fifth of the gross national product. This burden is a source of growing political as well as financial strain on Turkey's relations with its Western allies.

Turkey today desperately needs both political stability and bold economic planning to revitalize its economy. It is exploring the possibilities of Common Market association as a means of obtaining both stimulus and support for internal economic reforms and progress.

AUSTRIA

Once a leading power in Central Europe, Austria today is a small, unified, and neutral free nation. Neutralization was the Russian price for withdrawing foreign occupation forces from the country in 1955. The Soviet Union, in relinquishing its hold over the country, hoped to counteract the affiliation of West Germany with NATO and to encourage neutralist trends in the rest of Europe. The Austrians, under mature and intelligent leadership, have taken their imposed neutrality seriously. They have been firm in resisting Soviet interference or influence in their internal affairs. An effective coalition of clerical and socialist parties has given the country a high degree of political stability since World War II. The government's major efforts have been directed at building the type of state found in Scandinavia. Austria's main external problems have focused on a dispute with Italy over the protection of Austrian minorities in the South Tyrol. Italy, for its part, has been anxious to forestall the growth of any irredentist movements in the region. Austria is keenly aware, however, that its independence is largely conditioned by the need to maintain satisfactory relations with the Soviet Union.

From 1815 to 1848, Austria had dominated European politics as the leading power of the German Confederation as well as of the Holy Alliance (Austria, Russia, and Prussia). In the second half of the 19th century, it was forced out of the political affairs of Germany and Italy, but tried to shore up its growing weakness by uniting with Hungary under one ruler. The rise of a nationalistic Slavic movement in the empire, though suppressed, led to the assassination, in 1914, of Archduke Francis Ferdinand, heir to the Austrian throne. The Austrian monarchy collapsed in World War I. The present boundaries of Austria, which was forbidden any kind of political or economic union with Germany, were fixed in 1919.

Inflation, starvation, chronic unemployment, financial scandals and crises, and growing political unrest plagued the country in the years following World War I. Sharp internal discord (the two major political parties built their own private armies) greatly weakened the country in the face of growing Nazi power in Germany. Efforts to keep Austria independent failed in 1938 when German troops entered the country and annexed it to the German Reich. At the close of World War II the country was divided into American, British, French, and Soviet zones of occupation, and a provisional Austrian government was formed. After more than eight years of negotiation, the country was finally re-established as an independent and democratic state.

Mindful of the lessons of the 1930's, Austria's major political forces (primarily the People's party and the Socialist party) joined in a cooperative effort to rebuild the country. The two parties share the political offices of the government and are required to endorse jointly all bills submitted to parliament. They have succeeded in checking inflation and in promoting rapid economic expansion. With effective governmental leadership, the country has achieved prosperity with stability.

Austrian industry, the most important sector of the economy, has more than doubled its production since the end of World War II. It is less dependent on imports of raw materials than before the war and in a stronger position to export. Almost every year, new records are being set in industrial and mineral production, government revenues and expenditures, exports and imports, tourist income, exchange reserves, employment, and bank deposits and advances. Principal industries include: textiles, machinery and vehicles, iron and steel, chemicals and products, finished metal products, paper, and electrical machinery and equipment. Modernization, greatly assisted by American aid, has improved the competitive position of many industries. Small businesses and craft trades have declined in relative importance, though the country is still famous for its skilled craftsmen (glass blowers, jewelers, goldsmiths, potters, lace makers, wood carvers, and stone cutters).

Although only 21 percent of the total land area is farmed, Austria today produces a greater amount of food than in prewar years with less manpower. Efficient cultivation, fertilizers, better seeding, and rapid progress in electrification (Austria is one of the foremost producers of hydroelectric power in Europe) have helped to make the country 87 percent self-sufficient in foodstuffs. About two-thirds of total agricultural production is devoted to dairying and livestock breeding.

West Germany, Italy, and the United States are Austria's major trading partners today—an important change from the prewar pattern dominated by traditional markets in the east and southeast. Austria is required, however, to ship a million tons of crude oil annually to the Soviet Union as part of reparations until 1965. This has imposed some economic strains on the country. Although Austria is one of the largest oil producers in Europe, the free deliveries to the USSR leave little, if any, for export.

Austria's relations with the Common Market countries present difficulties similar to those facing Finland. The Soviet Union has warned Austrians that their association with the European Economic Community would constitute a violation of their postwar treaty obligations. Economically, however, the country can ill afford to risk permanent exclusion from the Community, and Austrian authorities have been outspoken in their insistence that some kind of association with the Common Market is essential for the country's continued prosperity.

SWITZERLAND

The oldest republic in the world, Switzerland shares close ties with the West but is deeply committed to a long-standing policy of armed neutrality. Located in the heart of Europe, it has been a traditional haven for refugees. A multilingual state with four national languages (German, French, Italian, and Romansh), it is nevertheless well integrated. It maintains a small but well-trained army as a backing for its posture of confidence and hard-headed independence. The country participates in the activities of several

United Nations agencies but is not directly a member of the United Nations. It has long played host, however, to various international organizations.

The Swiss, stemming originally from German, French, and Italian ethnic groups, have enjoyed independence since the 14th century, when various cantons joined to form a Swiss Confederation. In the mid-17th century they received formal international recognition. At the end of the Napoleonic wars, in 1815, the Congress of Vienna recognized perpetual Swiss neutrality. The country remained neutral during the two world wars. The Confederation today is a federal republic governed under a constitution adopted in 1848 and revised in 1874. About 94 percent of the present population is native born.

Switzerland lacks minerals and other raw materials and is limted in its agricultural potential owing to a lack of level and fertile land. Imports of food and fodder and of industrial raw materials are financed with exports of manufactured goods. Swiss manufactures, emphasizing quality of workmanship rather than quantity, are the mainstay of the economy; they employ about 46 percent of the entire labor force. Important Swiss industries include: machinery (ranging from heavy arms and ammunition to fine precision and optical instruments), textiles, and chemicals. Watches and machinery account for about 40 percent of all Swiss export value.

Transportation, insurance, tourism, and international banking are other important branches of the economy. Income from these more than compensates for Switzerland's traditional foreign-trade deficit. The country is one of the world's largest insurance centers. Its strong financial position also makes it a favorite bank depository with persons throughout the world. Preserving the secrecy of individual bank depositors is a jealously guarded tradition. Foreign deposits and other assets in Switzerland have been estimated at a value of several billion dollars. Swiss assets abroad (such as investments in foreign corporations, real estate, or insurance) are equally large.

Stable political and social conditions contribute much to the remarkable stability of Switzerland's economy. Internal issues revolve primarily around questions of social welfare, state participation in industry, centralization of governmental power, and woman's suffrage (approved by only two Swiss cantons in 1959). The chief political parties and the people as a whole are joined in firm support of a strong national defense (traditionally the largest expenditure in the national budget). A well-trained citizen's militia, the Swiss army is composed of four army corps (including independent mountain brigades), an air force, and special troops. Military service is obligatory for males from 20 to 60 years of age. The country can muster an estimated 480,000 trained troops in peacetime.

This military force is an important element in Switzerland's sense of fiber and independence. It is more than a symbol, however, since there is little question that the country would try to resist any conventional aggression. At the same time, however, Switzerland is not today an object of serious foreign rivalries or ambitions. Indeed, its neutrality under present world conditions is as useful to foreign interests as to its own. With Austria and Sweden, it is ready to consider some form of economic association with the Common Market which would respect this neutrality.

WEST GERMANY

The Federal Republic of Germany under Chancellor Konrad Adenauer has risen from rubble and defeat to become transfigured as Western Europe's most confident, prosperous, and powerful country. West Germany's remarkable resurgence since World War II is based on a dramatic enlargement of German national horizons to embrace the interests and problems of Western Europe as a whole. Its rapprochement with France, after three centuries of conflict, is the keystone of its progress as a full partner in a peaceful and stable community of nations. For the 53 million Germans in the west, separation from 17 million Germans in the east remains a great issue but has helped to strengthen the movement for Western

Europe's regional integration. By playing on hopes for eventual re-unification of Germany as a whole, the Soviet Union may in time be able to arrest the momentum of the movement. Much will depend, however, on the character of West German politics and policies under whatever political leadership succeeds the almost personal rule that has shaped the German Federal Republic since its inception. Dr. Adenauer reached the age of 86 in January 1962. Uncertainty about his successor casts a large question mark on the direction his country will take in the future.

Divided into many territorial units from the 17th to the 19th centuries, Germany emerged as Europe's strongest industrial power between 1871 (when Prussia defeated France) and World War I. Following the war, Germany became a republic under the liberal Weimar constitution. Adolf Hitler and the National Socialist (Nazi) party converted the country into a dictatorship in 1933. Complete defeat in World War II led to the division of Germany into four occupation zones. West Germany (consisting of the former British, French, and American zones) was proclaimed a federal republic in 1949, pending a final peace settlement. The city of Berlin, inside East Germany, was divided into administrative zones and soon reflected the Cold War division of Germany and Europe as a whole. West Germany was freed of occupation controls and became fully independent in 1955.

Until a peace treaty permits the establishment of a unified government for Germany, the Federal Republic is governed under a constitution adopted in 1949. A bicameral legislature (the Bundesrat and Bundestag) and an executive (whose powers are vested in a chancellor) form the federal government. Members of the Bundestag are elected for four-year terms by universal, free, and secret ballot; they include nonvoting deputies representing West Berlin. Members of the Bundesrat are appointed by provincial governments according to population and enjoy veto power over legislation affecting the provinces. Both the executive and the legislature may introduce legislation into the Bundestag. The chancellor elected by a majority of the Bundestag, is the leader of the executive branch. He serves until a majority vote dismisses him, or until a new Bundestag is elected. A president, elected for a five-year term by a federal convention, serves as chief of state (promulgating laws and receiving foreign ambassadors). West Berlin is governed under its own constitution adopted in 1950. A lord mayor, elected by a house of representatives, determines the general policy of the city government.

Considerable aid from Western nations since World War II has helped to make the Federal Republic one of the world's great industrial powers. From 1950 to 1959 the gross national product rose from $23.1 billion to $58.4 billion. Manufacturing industries and services have contributed the largest share of this increase. Purchasing power and living standards are high and the country's currency, one of the hardest in Europe, enjoys a strong position.

West Germany has five major industrial installations (in addition to the West Berlin industrial center): metallurgical, chemical, textile, and consumer industries in the Ruhr-Westphalia complex; automotive, chemical, and other industries in the Upper Rhine Valley; mechanical industries in southern Germany; ship-building industries in the Bremen and Hamburg areas; and automotive and other industries in central Germany. Coal deposits and reserves, the most important in Western Europe, are found in the Saar and Aachen-Ruhr areas. The Federal Republic leads Western Europe as a producer of electric power (generated primarily by thermal plants fueled by hard coal) as well as a steel producer (29,436,000 metric tons in 1959).

Most transportation and communications facilities and utilities are publicly owned. In addition, the federal government has substantial holdings in thousands of enterprises, including iron and steel works, coal and lignite mines, and engineering, aluminum, and chemical plants. In general, however, government economic policy has sought to encourage free enterprise with a minimum of state control. The government's major economic problems have been defense expenditures, contributions to Berlin relief expenditures, and the question of controlling cartels.[1] Commitments to NATO in the form of armed forces and armaments place a heavy burden on the economy. Economic support of West Berlin has exceeded by several times the amount of taxes collected in the city. Cartels, finally, are a long-standing problem in Germany and extremely difficult to control.

Although overshadowed by industry in economic importance, agriculture and forestry claim 87 percent of the Federal Republic's total area. Some 6 million people are engaged in farming. Most farmers are landowners (only 875,000 are hired hands). Grain, root vegetables, fodder, and garden produce are among the chief crops. The country is also renowned for fruit crops and as a producer of wines. While producing 70 percent of its wheat needs, West Germany must import about 27 percent of its food requirements.

West Germany today is one of the world's great trading nations. Importing agricultural products, raw materials, and fuels, it exports primarily finished manufactured goods (principally machines and machine tools, chemicals, motor vehicles, aircraft, and ships). The United States is its chief trading partner, followed by France, the Netherlands, Belgium-Luxembourg, Sweden, Italy, Austria, and the United Kingdom. Exports to Asia and Latin America have been increasing in recent years, a trend accompanied by large foreign investments in South and Central America and elsewhere.

The broad objectives of the Federal Republic—economic growth and close cooperation with the West—have the support of the major political parties in the country. On specific internal and external policies, however, disagreements are growing. Governmental participation in the economy, trade with East Germany and the communist bloc, defense of Western rights in Berlin, negotiations for German reunification, and matters of national defense are among the main issues. Controversy may become particularly sharp in the

[1] Combinations of firms to fix prices, limit supply, divide markets, etc. The cartel, of German origin, achieved prominence in the world depression of the 1870's, which coincided with the unification of Germany and the growth of its economy.

field of defense. As a member of NATO, West Germany is committed to an armed force build-up of 350,000 men by 1962, equipped with a growing variety of missiles under American control. In some quarters, this build-up is opposed both as an economic strain and as a provocation to the Soviet Union. Other groups are pressing for greater West German control over missiles in order to give the country an independent deterrent capability. Internal debate on this issue, if permitted an open eruption, could strain West Germany's relations with the United States and compound its difficulties with the Soviet bloc.

NETHERLANDS

A constitutional monarchy, the Kingdom of the Netherlands is a staunch NATO supporter. It is deeply committed to the principle of collective security and was the first country in the world to enact constitutional provisions for yielding authority to supranational organizations. The country has made an outstanding recovery from World War II. Rotterdam, nearly wiped out by Nazi air attack in 1940, is today the second largest port in the world. The Netherlands, joined with Belgium and Luxembourg in the Benelux Economic Union, enjoys an exceptionally high standard of living. It is greatly dependent, however, on foreign economic developments over which it has little or no control. Although suffering relatively few changes domestically since the 1930's, the country has become the target of anti-colonial pressures overseas. The Netherlands Antilles (two groups of islands in the West Indies) and Surinam (Netherlands Guiana on the north coast of South America) were granted equality with the Netherlands homeland in 1954, with complete internal autonomy and a share in the government of the kingdom. Netherlands New Guinea (the western part of New Guinea termed West Irian by Indonesians) remained under Dutch control when sovereignty was granted to the Republic of Indonesia in 1949. Indonesia, however, has asserted its right to the territory. As in the case of Portugal, the free-world support which the Netherlands has been able to muster in defense of its overseas interests strongly colors the country's present international attitudes.

In the 17th century, under the leadership of Holland, the provinces of the Netherlands were united as the leading commercial and maritime power in the world. Conquest by France in 1795 ended a century of gradual decay. The Kingdom of the Netherlands was established by the great powers of Europe at the Congress of Vienna in 1815. A revolt by the southern provinces in 1830 led to the establishment of Belgium as a separate kingdom. The Netherlands, neutral during World War I, was unable to maintain neutrality in World War II. The country underwent severe destruction and repression until liberated by Allied forces in 1945.

The Dutch economy is both agricultural and industrial. Natural resources are limited. Nearly all industries depend on the importation of raw materials for processing finished products for export. Food-processing, textile, metallurgical, chemical, wood-finishing, and oil-refining industries are particularly important. Agriculture is equally vital. More than one-third of total agricultural production is exported. The country's geographical position on the sea, providing excellent harbor facilities and numerous internal waterways, also enables service industries (such as banks, trading companies, shipping enterprises, and brokerage and supply firms) to play a major role in the economy.

Much of the land is below sea level, reclaimed and protected by dykes. Although one-third of the total land area is under crops, the soil is frequently poor. Farms are small but worked intensively. Large regions consist of moist grassland. This has led to the development of large-scale livestock raising and dairying. The Netherlands is a major exporter of eggs, cheese, condensed milk, ham, and bacon. It is also famous as a flower-growing center, specializing in tulips and other bulbs grown for the export trade.

The country has made substantial progress in industrialization since the beginning of this century. The Royal Dutch Shell Oil Company and the Philips Electrical Company (the greatest electrical products firm in Europe) are striking examples of phenomenal success. Since World War II, the progress of the metallurgical industry has been particularly great. These developments are reflected in the pattern of the country's foreign trade, increasing in industrial products and decreasing in food products and foodstuffs. Enjoying monetary equilibrium and a favorable balance of payments, the Netherlands can look forward to a period of continuing economic expansion.

Through its economic union with Belgium and Luxembourg, the Netherlands is able to draw on the advantages of an integrated economic area that continues to have large industrial possibilities. These three countries, as a unit, provide the Common Market with one of its most vital economic underpinnings (see Chapter 3). Hedged in between West Germany and France, they also have adopted the role of serving as the Common Market's unofficial conscience and defender of the original purpose and spirit of the Treaty of Rome.

BELGIUM

Poor in natural resources except coal, the Kingdom of Belgium has successfully exploited its geographic position, excellent transport facilities, and immense raw materials from overseas territories to become the most highly industrialized country in Europe. After World War II, Belgium gave the movement for European unity some of its most outstanding spokesmen (Brussels serves as the headquarters of Euratom and the Common Market). In recent years, however, it has found it increasingly difficult to keep pace with the economic and political evolution of the non-European world.

The Belgian nation today is seeking to absorb both the dislocative effects of internal modernization and the profound shocks to its recent colonial interests in the Congo basin of Africa. Plagued by unemployment and increased competition in world markets, the government has taken various measures to modernize plants and to create new industries. Mergers of small or outmoded industrial plants and the closing of less productive coal mines have generated widespread discontent. Overseas, the precipitous decision to free the

Belgian Congo (1960) unleashed a whirlwind of forces that plunged the region into chaos.

Some of Belgium's wealth and substance as a European power had its source in the Congo (explored and settled at the end of the 19th century). About three-fourths of all Congolese business was controlled by five Belgian holding companies, a concentration of economic power without parallel in modern times. Growing tension and fear of bloodshed inspired Belgium to grant the territory independence, but with little or no preparation for an orderly transition of power and administration. Hopes for some stability were placed in the emergence of a pro-Belgian rump government in Katanga (the economic heart of the Congo), but were quickly dealt a series of shattering blows. The role of the United Nations in the troubled affairs of the territory, rent by tribal factionalism, introduced a disturbing element in the Atlantic Alliance. Despite Belgium's international outlook and commitments, neutralism is a strong undercurrent in the nation's internal politics.

Sustained largely by foreign trade, Belgium exports some 50 percent of its industrial output. Iron and steel, textiles, machinery, nonferrous metals, and diamonds have been leading exports. A wide range of products are also manufactured by the chemical industry. With the loss of the Congo, important both as a supplier of raw materials and a market for Belgian products, trade with European countries and with the Western Hemisphere can be expected to expand. Sizable quantities of bread and feed grains, fodder concentrates, and fruits must be imported. Livestock production, the most important sector of Belgian agriculture, enables the country to meet about 94 percent of its meat requirements and to be self-sufficient in butter, milk, and eggs.

LUXEMBOURG

The Grand Duchy of Luxembourg (a constitutional monarchy) consists of some 320,000 tenaciously nationalistic people who speak French and German in addition to their own dialect and who possess a well-established steel industry and a high standard of living. Despite its negligible armed forces (about 2,000 men), the country is an original member of NATO. Highly industrialized, it serves as the headquarters of the European Coal and Steel Community. Strong support of European integration does not prevent Luxembourgers from insisting on their individuality as a nation that has survived a long history of foreign domination. The sense of ethnic distinctiveness is expressed in a national motto: "We want to remain what we are."

Historically, this feeling can be traced back to the year 963, when a certain Count Sigefroid reconstructed a small ruined fortress on the site of Luxembourg's present capital. Trebling in size, the territory became a duchy in the 14th century. From the 15th to the 19th centuries it was ruled successively by Spain, Austria, France, and the Netherlands. Belgium acquired more than half of its territory in 1839. Luxembourg became an independent and neutral state, under the protection of the great powers, in 1867. It was occupied by Germany in both world wars. A 1942 revolt protesting compulsory service in the German army met savage repression.

Many thousands of Luxembourgers emigrated to the United States and other countries during the 19th century. In 1870, however, rich deposits of iron ore were discovered in the country's southern region. A period of industrialization and prosperity followed, attracting many persons from neighboring countries. As a result, the population now includes many people of French, Belgian, or German ancestry. Luxembourg today has the largest proportion of foreign residents of any European country (about 15 percent of the population). About 20 percent of the labor force is composed of industrial workers (particularly miners and iron workers) of foreign birth. A dwindling of native farm workers (numbering less than a thousand in 1954) forced the government to appeal to the Netherlands for agricultural laborers in 1956.

Luxembourg's coalition governments since World War II have tried to pursue a policy of full employment and industrial diversification in order to reduce the country's dependence on its iron and steel industry. Tax concessions and special regulations were devised to attract foreign firms. Manufacturing accounts for over two-fifths of the country's gross national product (compared to less than one-tenth for agriculture). More than 70 percent of total industrial production and close to 90 percent of total exports are accounted for by steel alone. Fluctuations in the demand for steel thus greatly influence the prosperity of the entire economy. Conversely, as a major steel producer, the tiny country occupies an important position in the world economy.

Luxembourg exports over four-fifths of its total industrial output. In addition to iron and steel products, this includes leather goods, beer, dairy products, tobacco, wood, and cement. Both the government and private industry, joined in a Board of Industrial Development, are committed to strengthening the country's medium industry branches. Oil, coal, cotton and linen, food products, cars, and agricultural machinery are among the chief imports. Belgium, West Germany, France, the Netherlands, Switzerland, and the Scandinavian countries comprise Luxembourg's principal trading partners.

FRANCE

The dominant influence shaping France today is General de Gaulle. Rallying the nation during World War II, resigning as head of the French government in 1946, and returning to avert the threat of civil war in 1958, de Gaulle assumed leadership of the country's fifth republic since the French Revolution with a driving ambition to re-fashion France into a first-class power. As with West Germany's Dr. Adenauer, de Gaulle's vision of a strong France (with its own nuclear deterrent) is blended with a broader vision of a strong and united European community—in de Gaulle's case perhaps stretching, eventually, from the Atlantic to the Urals. Unlike Dr. Adenauer, de Gaulle has less assurance that his nation possesses the institutional strengths necessary to move forward without his personal leadership. It is debatable how long the country will remain responsive to the de Gaulle "mystique." As though aware that he will have to leave the public scene in the not-distant future, de Gaulle has devoted a major share of his energy to resolving France's bitter conflicts in Algeria so that the nation can work for its greater future at least united and at peace with itself.

France's postwar history consists of a long series of political vicissitudes. De Gaulle withdrew from the government he helped establish during the war primarily over the issue of executive powers. In spite of his opposition, the Fourth Republic was launched in 1946 under a constitution which concentrated almost all powers in the lower house of Parliament (the National Assembly). The proliferation of parties in the Assembly, characteristic of French politics, prevented the formation of stable majority and minority blocs. Diverse political groups displayed little readiness to recognize the right of opposition or to cooperate with those in power. French governments suffered an increasingly precarious tenure. In the meantime, almost continuous fighting overseas coupled with an unbroken succession of retreats and defeats led to deep disillusionment, especially within the French army, with parliamentary governments. Willingly or forcibly, France eventually relinquished over 3 million square miles of formerly colonial territory. Humiliation in Morocco, Tunisia, Indochina, and elsewhere spurred a group of army officers in Algeria, aided by French settlers, to make a determined effort not to suffer another defeat. Losing patience with civilian leadership in Paris, they seized control of Algiers in 1958. Sympathetic movements spread to Corsica and parts of the French homeland. The government found itself powerless, and a right-wing coup seemed imminent.

As the only French leader commanding genuine national loyalty, de Gaulle was quickly installed as premier and succeeded in restoring the authority of the central government. A new constitution, providing for a strong executive, was submitted to a national referendum in the fall of 1958. Overwhelmingly approved, it established the Fifth Republic with de Gaulle as its first president. The new constitution also created the concept of the French Community—a fusion of France proper and its overseas departments, colonies, and other territories. The overseas territories were given the choice of severing all ties with France (including considerable economic aid) or entering the new community. Most of the territories voted to remain in the French community. Algeria, however, became the battlefield of a protracted civil war.

Economically, France enjoyed a more happy history. Postwar reconstruction and development, supported by substantial American aid and guided by the comprehensive Monnet Plan, progressed rapidly. The European Coal and Steel Community, in which France joined, stimulated the expansion of heavy industry. By 1948 or 1949, economic recovery had been substantially completed. The 1950's brought a period of unprecedented prosperity as the economy continued to expand. The economic climate, superior to that of the best interwar years, owed much to the inventiveness of French engineers and industrial designers, the existence of a highly trained labor force, the skill of financial leaders and economists in the government, and a varied resource base.

The country faced the danger of economic disaster briefly in 1958. Most of its foreign reserves had been spent. In an effort to reduce budget deficits, improve the balance of payments, and strengthen the currency, the de Gaulle government launched a "partial austerity" program. The franc was devalued, thereby suppressing export subsidies and freeing imports. Various subsidies to industries were cut while the prices of coal, gas, electricity, and railway fares were raised. The tax system was reformed, and tax rates were increased. Official prices were set for certain foodstuffs. A great expansion of trade had taken place by 1960 (as a result of the lowering of tariff barriers under the European Economic Community) and the government now felt ready to push a program for expanded agricultural and industrial production.

France is richly endowed in terms of balanced natural resources. Its thriving farm economy is based on a favorable climate, extensive areas of rich soil, and a long-established tradition of skilled agriculture. The French industrial complex is one of Europe's oldest as well as one of its most modern. Standards of industrial workmanship are traditionally high. Deposits of iron ore are large, and domestic reserves of natural gas are important. Hydroelectric and thermoelectric plants compose a well-integrated network. The French Community overseas also contributes considerable resources. Large reserves of petroleum and natural gas in the Sahara, jeopardized by the possible loss of Algeria, are particularly important for the country's future economic growth. Until recently, France's total reliance on imports of Middle Eastern oil has constituted a heavy drain on its foreign exchange reserves. The government expects that petroleum from the Sahara will make France self-sufficient in this resource by 1963, with good possibilities for future export.

Agriculture, a vital sector of the economy, employs over one-fourth of the country's labor force. The most important agricultural products are cereals, industrial crops, root crops, and wines. Although the de Gaulle government abolished agricultural subsidies in 1958, wheat producers and wine growers have been a strong influence in the maintenance of price supports and tariff protection. The value of French agricultural exports is second only to that of the Netherlands. Rural improvement programs include increased mechanization and a consolidation of small, scattered landholdings that had become fragmented as a result of the French law providing for equal rights of inheritance.

The expansion of French industry has been notable since World War II. One of the leaders of Europe in ferrous metallurgy, France ranks fifth in the world in steel production and fourth in aluminum as well as textiles, the most important consumer-goods industry. It also boasts the third largest automotive industry in Europe. Many industries have pioneered in technological advance. Firms wanting to relocate, reconvert, or modernize their plants are eligible for governmental subsidies and easy credit. At the same time, many branches of industry are still reluctant to adopt modern techniques of mass production.

As is to be expected, heavy imports of fuels, raw materials for industry, and industrial machinery characterize France's foreign trade. Overseas territories of the French Community generally furnish about one-fourth of all French imports. The export trade consists chiefly of manufactures, chemicals (ranging from perfumes to sulfuric acid), and foodstuffs. European countries, overseas territories, and the United States are among France's chief trade partners.

French politics remains the major cloud casting uncertainty on the nation's future. In the field of foreign policy, the desire to pursue an independent course is pronounced. De Gaulle has not concealed his distaste for the United Nations or his displeasure with NATO and American policies. Domestically, the tensions that characterize French political rivalries have become somewhat obscured by pressing immediate problems, but they remain unresolved. The Parliament of the Fifth Republic—trying to overcome political fragmentation—has made an effort to divide the National Assembly into "government" and "opposition" blocs along the lines of British practice. With or without de Gaulle, it is doubtful that this simplified alignment of forces will hold fast in light of the expediency and gnostic sectarianism that characterize French political life.

III   *The Common Market*

Wₙₜₕ over 169 million people, the European
Economic Community (EEC) represents a powerful combination
of material and human resources. As a unit, it is the world's largest
importer and the world's second largest producer of automobiles,
steel, and coal. Excluding associated territories overseas, the Common Market is about one-eighth as large (450,000 square miles)
and almost as populous as the United States. Taken as a single
economic unit, it is ahead of the Soviet Union and second to the
United States in industrial production. Its potential for further
economic progress has been underscored by an exceptionally high
rate of economic growth in recent years. Germany, Belgium, and
Luxembourg are the most highly industrialized of the Six. Italy,
least developed in the south, continues to lean heavily on its agricultural base, despite the growth of industry in the north. France
and the Netherlands fall between these poles. The Netherlands,
Belgium, Luxembourg, and the Ruhr in Western Germany are the
most densely populated (900 people per square mile in the Netherlands, compared to 60 in the United States).

Despite national and regional differences, the EEC countries are
economically more competitive than complementary; they sell over
a third of their exports to one another. The similarity of production patterns, usually permitting considerable room for specialization within any broad class of products, can be expected to encourage efficiency and lower unit costs through enhanced competition
for the opportunities provided by a growing mass market. A skilled
and industrious population, a favorable governmental and business

environment, and a highly developed tradition of international trade are among the Common Market's greatest strengths. While only moderately endowed with natural resources, the EEC countries look forward to developing mutually beneficial relationships with the associated countries and territories overseas, which possess enormous reserves.

It is difficult to convey the Common Market's historical significance because established concepts do not adequately encompass the nature of the entity that is being formed. Discussions centering on issues of supranationality versus sovereignty miss the actual functioning of the EEC's institutions. Member states are still pursuing national ends, but through mechanisms which enable them to transcend the mounting limitations on their ability to act independently. In this sense, the European Economic Community is not destroying but enhancing the capacity of nations to influence and direct their own economic and political development.

THE TREATY OF ROME

Observers have likened the Treaty of Rome to the United States Constitution in historic import. It has already had a far-reaching psychological and ideological impact, firing the imagination of political leaders in Latin America, Asia, and Africa. As with the founding of the United States, the new organization has still to work out a balance between its centripetal and centrifugal forces, and much of its vitality will depend on how its basic document is interpreted and carried out.

A brief summary of the treaty, while inadequate as a description of so formidable an undertaking, may help to indicate the magnitude of the EEC's objectives.

The broad mission of the Common Market is defined as promoting "the harmonious development of economic activities, continuous and balanced expansion, increased stability, a more rapid improvement in the standard of living, and closer relations between its member states."

The member states are committed to the following:

1. Removal of customs duties and import and export quotas between each other.
2. Establishment of a common tariff and commercial policy for states outside the Community.
3. Abolition within the Community of obstacles to the free movement of persons, services, and capital.
4. Inauguration of common agricultural and transport policies.
5. Establishment of a system insuring competition.
6. Adoption of procedures for coordination of domestic policies and for remedying balance-of-payments disequilibria.
7. Removal of differences in national laws necessary for operation of the Common Market.
8. Creation of a European social fund to educate and train displaced workers and to raise their standard of living.
9. Establishment of a European investment bank to facilitate economic expansion.
10. Association of dependent overseas territories with the Community.

As the institutions of the Community (see Figure 2), the treaty established an Assembly, a Council, a Commission, and a Court of Justice. An advisory Economic and Social Committee was formed to assist the Council and the Commission.

The Assembly, composed initially of 142 members appointed by and from the national Parliaments, is required to prepare proposals for election of its members by direct universal suffrage and uniform procedures. Its major responsibility is to review (but not reject) Council and Commission proposals in cases provided by the treaty. It is empowered to censure the Commission and force it to resign by a two-thirds majority of those present and an absolute majority of the membership.

The Council, composed of one representative from each Government, is responsible for coordinating the general economic policies of member states. In general, this body "exercises the powers of de-

FIGURE 2

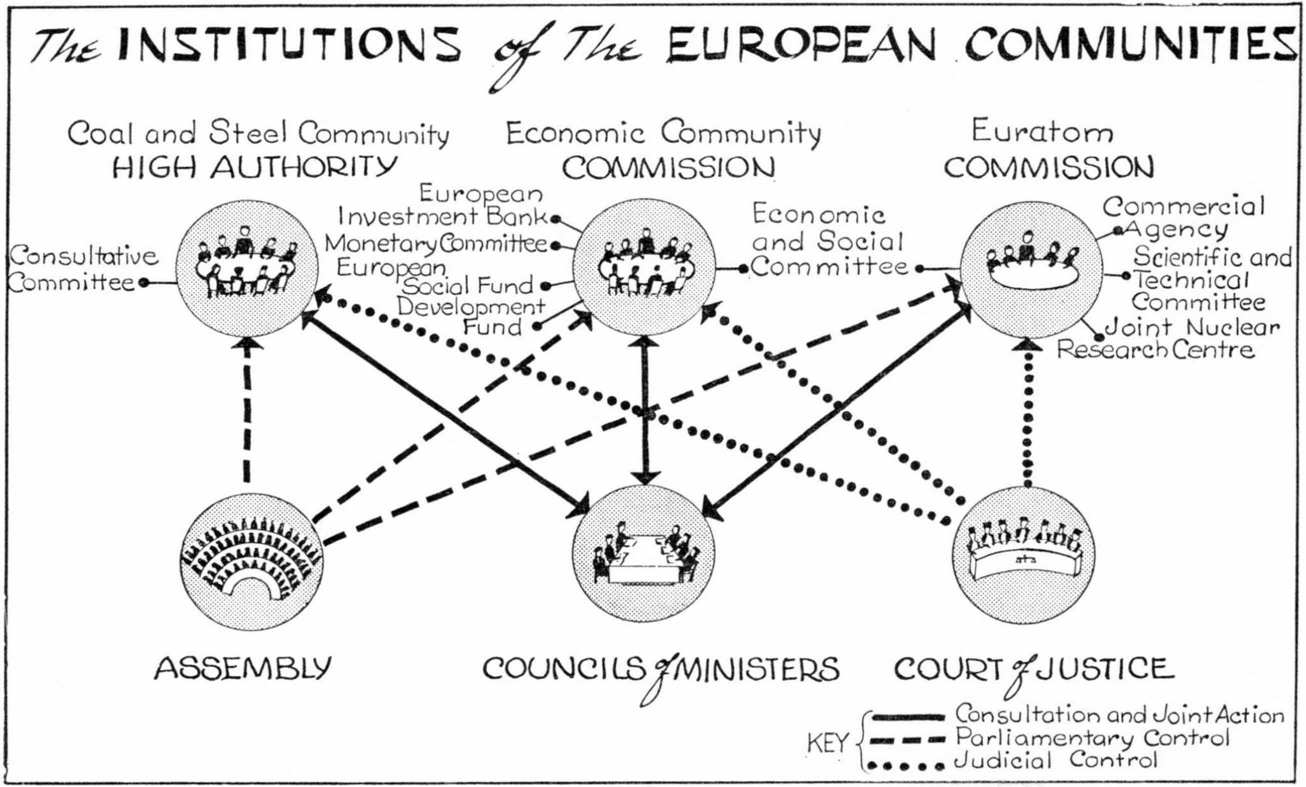

The INSTITUTIONS *of The* EUROPEAN COMMUNITIES

Coal and Steel Community
HIGH AUTHORITY

Economic Community
COMMISSION

Euratom
COMMISSION

Commercial
Agency
Scientific and
Technical
Committee
Joint Nuclear
Research Centre

Economic
and Social
Committee

European
Investment Bank
Monetary Committee
European
Social Fund
Development
Fund

Consultative
Committee

COUNCILS *of* MINISTERS

COURT *of* JUSTICE

ASSEMBLY

KEY
{
Consultation and Joint Action
Parliamentary Control
Judicial Control
}

cision." Decisions are taken by a simple majority except where provided otherwise. In cases requiring weighted votes, the following weights are used: France, Germany, and Italy 4 votes each; Belgium and the Netherlands 2 each; and Luxembourg 1. Twelve votes are required in the case of decisions to be made on proposals of the Commission.

The Commission, consisting of nine members appointed by common agreement, is responsible to the Community as a whole rather than to any individual government. It has three main responsibilities:

(1) to supervise the application of treaty provisions and of measures adopted by the organs of the Community;

(2) to formulate recommendations or opinions in regard to matters covered by the treaty, in cases where this is explictly provided or where the Commission deems it necessary; and

(3) to enjoy independent powers of decision in certain instances and take part in the preparation of decisions by the Council and Assembly. Appointed for four years and eligible for reappointment, Commissioners are required to devote their full time to their duties and prohibited from engaging in any other professional activity. Subject to removal by a vote of censure of the Assembly, a Commissioner can also be removed for cause by decision of the Court of Justice on petition from either the Council or the Commission itself.

The Court of Justice consists of seven judges selected by common agreement and appointed for six years. The Court's major function is to adjudicate disputes arising under the treaty. Responsible for reviewing the legality of decisions (but not of recommendations or opinions) of the Council and the Commission, the Court can hear complaints or appeals against the decisions of a Community organ by the Council, the Commission, member states, corporations, or individuals. The Court may also hear cases involving alleged violations of articles in the treaty by member states.

Both the Court of Justice and the Assembly were established under the treaty as common institutions for the three European

Communities: the Coal and Steel Community, Euratom, and the Common Market.

The Economic and Social Committee was established as a consultative group consisting of 101 members, appointed by the Council, representing various branches of economic and social life. It includes producers, farmers, workers, businessmen, and professional men who serve for four-year terms. France, Italy, and Germany are allowed 24 representatives each; Belgium and the Netherlands 12 each; and Luxembourg 5. The Committee is organized into specialized sections which deal with the main fields of activity covered by the treaty, such as agriculture and transport. Its principal responsibility is to advise the Commission, although it may also be consulted by the Council.

Financial provisions of the Rome Treaty include an annual budget which is prepared by the Commission, submitted to the Council and the Assembly, and financed by the member states. France, Germany, and Italy each contribute 28 percent of the budget; Belgium and the Netherlands, 7.9 percent; and Luxembourg, 0.2 percent. The European Social Fund is separately financed as a distinct activity, but its receipts and expenditures are included in the Community's annual budget. Looking forward to the possibility of an independent source of revenue in the future, the treaty requires the Commission to develop proposals for replacing government contributions by an independent Community tax system.

The treaty originally provided for a 12-year transition period, divided into three stages of four years each, for the gradual establishment of the Common Market. A unanimous vote in the Council is necessary to move from the first to the second stage. Failure to achieve unanimity can extend the first stage for one or two years, though at the end of the sixth year a decision must be sought through a majority vote of the Commission. In the face of persistent disagreement, any member state can at this point require the Council to appoint a three-man Arbitration Board whose decisions would be binding on all members.

The elimination of customs duties between member states and the establishment of a common customs tariff in relation to third countries are governed by a detailed but flexible time schedule. During the transition period, individual-country tariff rates are to be adjusted up or down toward the single common external tariff which, with certain exceptions, is to represent the arithmetic average of duties in four customs areas—Benelux, France, West Germany, and Italy.

A common agricultural policy, to be in full effect by the end of the transition, will have the purpose of increasing productivity, assuring an equitable standard of living to the agricultural population, stabilizing markets, guaranteeing supplies, and assuring reasonable consumer prices. It is contemplated that agricultural markets will be subject to various forms of regulation implemented by price controls, subsidies, stockpiling and carry-over systems, and other mechanisms.

Outlining the objectives of a common transport policy, the treaty anticipates that discrimination in rates and conditions will be abolished during the first two stages of the transition. Frontier taxes are to be reduced, and interstate traffic will be subject to common regulations. Carriers who are permitted to operate in member states will be allowed subsidies if necessary for the coordination of transport or the fulfillment of public service obligations.

By the end of the transition period, workers, businessmen, enterprises, and capital are to enjoy freedom of movement and establishment throughout the Community. Discrimination based on nationality in employment, wages, and other working conditions is to be eliminated. Cumulative social security benefits are to be payable anywhere in the Community.

As a policy of the Community, the treaty establishes rules and principles governing competition and provides for the "harmonization" of national laws and policies relating to fiscal and monetary matters. While monopolies are not outlawed, monopoly action inimical to the interests of other producers or consumers is forbidden. States are required to consult with each other and with the Commission on measures to be taken to counteract disturbing economic trends. With their foreign trade policies progressively coordinated during the transition, members of the Community are expected to act as a unit in international economic organizations. Negotiations with outside states after the transition are to be handled by the Commission, subject to the guidance and directives of the Council.

Social provisions of the treaty contemplate the eventual "harmonization of social systems." The Commission is directed to foster close collaboration between member states in the social field, with particular attention to: employment, labor laws and working conditions, vocational training, social welfare, safety measures against occupational accidents and diseases, industrial hygiene, trade-union laws, and collective bargaining.

A European Social Fund was established to improve employment possibilities and to increase the geographic and occupational mobility of labor in the Community. The Fund makes matching grants to member states for retraining, resettling, and compensating workers affected by economic dislocations resulting from liberalized trade policies and internal economic readjustments. The treaty also established a European Investment Bank to help finance projects in all sectors of the Community's economy, and an Overseas Development Fund to operate in the Community's overseas territories.

The colonies and overseas territories of the member states are associated with the Community for a five-year period, by which time subsequent arrangements are to be worked out by the Council. These territories are to enjoy the same tariff levels as the states themselves, but are also permitted to retain certain trade barriers for purposes of development and revenue.

The final articles of the treaty spell out the conditions under which the Community can enlarge its membership and broaden its association. Any European state may apply for membership by addressing an application to the Council. After consulting with the Commission, the Council must act by unanimous vote. The agreement on the conditions of admission must then be submitted to all contracting states for ratification according to their respective constitutional rules. The Community may also establish an association with an outside country, a union of states, or an international organization. This requires agreements embodying reciprocal rights and obligations, joint actions, and special procedures. In such cases, the Council consults with the Assembly before concluding the agreements by unanimous vote. If required, however, treaty amendments must be ratified by all member states.

THE POLITICAL CHARACTER
OF THE COMMON MARKET

Despite the political overtones of the Rome Treaty, many outside observers—particularly in Britain and the United States—viewed the establishment of the European Economic Community primarily in commercial or economic terms. An apparent failure or unwillingness to recognize the Common Market as an essentially political movement contributed to persistent misunderstanding of its basic impetus and character. To some extent, this misunderstanding was fostered by official British policy, which tried to reduce the problem of Europe to a question of economic and commercial relations. At the same time, the energy with which the Six sought to develop their customs union helped to color various interpretations of the Common Market's ultimate impact on other nations.

The fact that EEC members aspire for something more than a mere customs union is generally understood, but there has been a tendency to assess these aspirations in terms of measures required to buttress the customs union's viability. The need to go beyond the limits of a customs union is sometimes explained along the following lines: the free movement of labor, capital, and enterprise is necessary to help disadvantaged industries and areas and disemployed workers to adjust to the hardships which the customs union would entail; collective restraints on discriminatory or restrictive governmental and private measures are required to prevent the benefits of the customs union from being frustrated or nullified by public or private action; coordination of national economic and social policies is dictated by the need to safeguard the customs union from the disruptive pressures of different national interests; finally, the benefits of increased trade and regional specialization in themselves may not be enough to inspire the enormous efforts involved in establishing a customs union, efforts which call for the stronger incentive of some sort of political vision.[1]

These arguments, however useful from an analytical standpoint, tend to divert attention from the driving motivation of the European movement. For the leaders of the movement, the question is not whether common policies or common political goals are necessary to make the customs union work. These ends are viewed as desirable both in themselves and as part of a larger purpose of which the customs union is only one manifestation.

The political character of this purpose has been repeatedly reaffirmed by leading executives of Community institutions, by the European Parliament, and by the individual governments involved. A communique issued by the heads of the six Community countries at the close of a "summit" meeting at Bonn in July 1961 expressed the spirit of their commitment as follows:

> The Heads of State or of Government of the Federal Republic of Germany, Belgium, France, Italy, Luxembourg, as well as the Prime Minister and Minister for Foreign Affairs of the Netherlands, desirous of affirming the spiritual values and political traditions which form their common heritage, united in awareness of the great tasks which Europe is called upon to fulfill within the community of free peoples in order to safeguard liberty and peace in the world, anxious to strengthen the political, economic, social and cultural ties which exist between their peoples, especially in the framework of the European Communities, and to advance toward the union of Europe;
>
> Convinced that only a united Europe, allied to the United States of America and to other free peoples, is in a position to face the dangers which menace the existence of Europe and of

[1] See Emile Benoit, *Europe at Sixes and Sevens,* New York: Columbia University Press, 1961, pp. 30-33.

the whole free world, and that it is important to unite the energies, capabilities and resources of all those for whom liberty is an inalienable possession; resolved to develop their political cooperation with a view to the union of Europe and to continue at the same time the work already undertaken in the European Communities;

Wishing for the adhesion to the European Communities of other European states ready to assume in all spheres the same responsibilities and the same obligations, have decided:

1. To give shape to the will for political union already implicit in the Treaties establishing the European Communities, and for this purpose to organize their cooperation, to provide for its development and to secure for it the regularity which will progressively create the conditions for a common policy and will ultimately make it possible to embody in institutions the work undertaken.

2. To hold, at regular intervals, meetings whose aim will be to compare their views, to concert their policies and to reach common positions in order to further the political union of Europe, thereby strengthening the Atlantic alliance. The necessary practical measures will be taken to prepare these meetings. In addition, the continuation of active cooperation among the Foreign Ministers will contribute to the continuity of the action undertaken in common. The cooperation of the Six must go beyond the political field as such, and will in particular be extended to the sphere of education, of culture and of research, where it will be ensured by periodical meetings of the Ministers concerned.

3. To instruct their Committee to submit to them proposals on the means which will as soon as possible enable a statutory character to be given to the union of their peoples.

The Heads of State or of Government are convinced that by thus organizing their cooperation, they will thereby further the application of the Rome and Paris Treaties. They also believe that their cooperation will facilitate those reforms which might seem opportune in the interests of the Communities' greater efficiency.[2]

The spirit of these goals has guided the development of the European Economic Community from its inception. Plans were developed, studies initiated, informational services established, regulations put into effect, surveys conducted, tariff and quota disarmament carried out, and a host of other problems faced in an atmosphere of anxiety to press the formulation of a common economic policy and to accelerate the transition period from 12 to 6 years. The drive to forge ahead as swiftly as possible brought into focus many of the critical issues on which the future of the Community will depend.

ISSUES CONFRONTING THE COMMUNITY

These issues include countless technical and political problems involved in the elimination of barriers to trade, in the development of a consensus for a common agricultural policy, in the formulation of programs for regional development and redevelopment both within and outside the Community, in the maintenance of a climate favorable to competition, in the establishment of adequate machinery to deal with monetary and fiscal crises, in the harmonization of social policies, in the evolution of vigorous and effective Community institutions, and in the development of healthy relations with the rest of the world.

In the field of trade, Common Market officials have consistently emphasized that the community will be "liberal" and "outward looking" in its policies. Nevertheless, outside countries have been greatly concerned about the possibility that the Community may seek increasing protection behind the wall of its customs union in the face of internal pressures. Some analysts feel that the Community's proposals for a common external tariff—an arithmetic average of the old tariffs of member countries—would lead to a

[2] Washington Bureau of the European Community Information Service, *Bulletin from the European Community,* No. 49, October 1961, p 6.

high degree of trade disruption and discrimination, since only Benelux had an originally low tariff. Others express anxiety that the Community may find itself reluctant to expedite the elimination of quantitive restrictions, or quotas, which often have served as a more effective barrier to trade than tariffs. Still others point to the knotty and elusive problem of eliminating less obvious but equally onerous obstructions to trade: import license laws affecting goods, the countries of origin, or the currency which can be used; charges which have an effect equivalent to customs duties; the substitution of internal taxes for customs duties; and the customs duty allowed by the Rome Treaty for the purpose of raising revenue.

In the area of achieving a common agricultural policy, the Community's difficulties are rooted in the structure of European agriculture and complicated by wide variations in the importance of agriculture in individual countries. The desire to attain self-sufficiency in agriculture was stimulated by two world wars. In many areas there is a pattern of fragmented land holdings, too small and too scattered for efficient operation. Many kinds of governmental intervention now exist to protect farm income: price-support schemes, export subsidies, equalization funds, commodity marketing agencies, and state trading. Agricultural productivity and prices vary widely in the member countries. In time, the Community hopes to arrive at uniform price levels and price supports through coordinated and integrated market organizations. This will entail structural reforms which may take a generation or more to accomplish.

Coupled to the problem of rural development is the gargantuan task of reducing the gaps between the Community's developed and underdeveloped areas. Massive infusions of investment will be required in several "hard core" areas where the per capita income is drastically below the Community average. The requirements of the Community's underdeveloped overseas territories, the present or potential needs of associated European states such as Greece and Turkey, and the growing obligation to provide increased aid to non-affiliated less-developed countries—all add to the staggering demands on the resources of the Common Market.

Maintaining the basic conditions of free and fair competition within the Community presents a set of different though equally challenging problems. Massive and subtle threats to the spirit of the Rome Treaty emanate from long-entrenched anticompetitve attitudes. Some observers feel that member states and important economic sectors have yet to demonstrate convincingly their support for the objective of free competition. Traditional private market-sharing agreements, if allowed to persist, could easily vitiate the hard-won steps of tariff and quota disarmament. Devising procedures for detecting restrictive practices and creating an effective enforcement machinery are among the most difficult tasks that Community officials must face.

Another serious issue centers on the capacity of the Community to withstand monetary and fiscal emergencies in one or more of its member states or to survive a prolonged world-wide or European recession. There is some question whether the Rome Treaty provides adequate equipment for dealing with such crises. Community officials are working hard to shape directives and programs to liberalize monetary and fiscal restrictions, to ease the movement of capital, and to coordinate domestic economic plans. In many areas, however, a unanimous vote of the Council is required to take action. Each country, moreover, is permitted, under the treaty, to take unilateral and protective measures if these are deemed essential to the national interest. In seeking to harmonize national budgetary and economic policies, the Community must rely primarily on the collaboration of member governments and their central banks and on mutual assistance in case of difficulties. Its ability to reconcile separate national needs with its own larger requirements is a fundamental question which will take a considerable time to resolve.

It also remains to be seen to what extent the Common Market will succeed in the formidable task of harmonizing social policies in such fields as employment, working conditions, wages, social security, health provisions, collective bargaining, labor mobility, and occupational training and relocation. Attempts to achieve greater equality in wages and social conditions have thus far been cautious.

The ways in which member states are approaching these problems are being studied so as to define the common ground that already exists.

Efforts to spur labor mobility have proven especially vexatious. A more rational redistribution of labor within the Community is urgently needed. In southern Italy, for example, about a million workers are in excess of foreseeable requirements. Plans to encourage large-scale migrations must cope with a variety of barriers: transportation costs, language and cultural differences, and strong local attachments. Even if these are surmounted, however, dramatic mass migrations may disrupt productivity in affected regions and create new problems. For the present, major attention in this field is being devoted to the more limited relocation of workers from poor crop areas to nearby industrial centers.

Perhaps the most crucial issue affecting the Community's future turns on the role that national differences will play in the shaping of its political character and structure. This involves not merely the persistence of rivalries between states, but also the divergent ways in which national objectives are related to the concept of European unity. For each member government, while broadly supporting the vision of a lasting concert of Europe, views the Common Market essentially as a vehicle for promoting its own long-range interests.

THE CHANNELING OF NATIONAL INTERESTS

West Germany looks upon the Common Market as a major means of restoring and strengthening Germany's position in Europe within the Western community of nations. Potentially, however, a conflict could arise between Western Germany's determination to resist Soviet pressure and its desire to prevent the permanent dismemberment of the German nation. Communist control of East Germany gives the Soviet Union a powerful lever for influencing both Germany and the European Community as a whole.

The Benelux countries see the Common Market as an indispensable instrument for safeguarding the rights and interests of smaller European Nations. It protects them from the drives and ambitions of surrounding powers, assures them a voice in European affairs, and provides them with an important measure of maneuverability in dealing with their larger neighbors.

France under General de Gaulle is hopeful the Common Market will help promote a historical resurgence of French power and influence both on the Continent and in the world. Franco-German amity is an essential prerequisite if France is to succeed in intensive internal efforts to revive its sense of greatness, purpose, and destiny.

Italy finds membership in the Common Market vital not only for promoting its own economic development but also for ensuring its political stability. It has the lowest per capita income of the Six and the largest and poorest of the Commmunity's underdeveloped regions. The country's political institutions have been subject to great strains. Common Market bonds furnish Italy considerable political as well as economic support as it seeks to build the foundations for stable national development.

Community members are joined in a conviction that their individual hopes and aspirations can best be realized through a commitment to common goals and institutions. They recognize the urgency of unity in order to prevent or control future Continental conflicts, to harness the enormous economic potential of their combined resources, and to strengthen Europe's independent influence in global affairs. Yet they approach these objectives from different national perspectives which constantly color and modify their common efforts.

An ambivalence pervades the entire Community. Tensions between "national" and "supranational" interests are visible on a number of levels: in the internal political dynamics of member states; in the rivalries among these states; in the relations between national governments and Community authorities; and in the relations of Community institutions with each other.

Currents of political thought in each of the Six reflect an ideological clash which is likely to grow in signifiance. Some, speaking more as "Europeans" than as nationals of a particular country, believe the Common Market's future rests on strengthening its supranational powers. Others insist the Community must rely for its continued vitality on the national states, which alone possess the ultimate powers of decision and action. In varying degrees, governmental policies within the Community are influenced by both points of view.

Official French pronouncements on internal and external Community matters tend to reject supranational concepts by stressing the importance of cooperation among strong governments. Displaying a marked preference for bilateral understandings and arrangements, France has cultivated close German political support, sought to reduce the importance of the Commission in Community negotiations with Great Britain, and pressed for closer political consultation among the foreign ministers of the Six outside the institutional framework of the Community.

French attitudes and policies, received sympathetically in the Federal Republic of Germany, encounter opposition among the Benelux countries. The smaller states view the Franco-German alliance with growing uneasiness. Fearful of being by-passed in vital policy decisions, they have resisted efforts to dilute the powers delegated to Community institutions, to shift Commission responsibilities to governments, or to transform the Community into an alliance of sovereign states.

Relations between the Commission and the Council of the Community are tinged with the same conflict. Whereas the Council speaks with the voices of the governments concerned, Commission officials have been outspoken defenders of their transcendent responsibilities to strengthen the Community institutionally. Their efforts to build the foundations of a supranational political structure are both resisted and supported by different elements of opinion in the Community at large.

The popular election of the Parliamentary Assembly, expected by 1963, may mark a decisive turning point in the Community's development. Some analysts anticipate a significant shift in the balance of power in the Community, weakening the Council and reinforcing the powers of the Commission. The elected Parliament might eventually even name the Council. Others feel that the stage is slowly being set for a complete integration of the three communities—the Common Market, Euratom, and the Coal and Steel Community—which already share common legal, statistical, and informational services as well as a common Assembly and Court of Justice.

Agitation for such a merger is growing. Influential pressure groups on the Continent have strongly urged that the three separate executive bodies of the Market, Euratom, and the Coal and Steel Authority be replaced by a single European Economic Executive Commission by 1962. It remains to be seen whether such pressure is able to overcome General de Gaulle's views on federation.

Despite various stresses and disagreements on the shape of ultimate objectives, however, all members of the Common Market are intent on implementing the Rome Treaty as quickly as possible. They are fearful of losing momentum, concerned that time may be working against them, and anxious to make the Common Market truly irreversible. Failure to develop rapidly, if coupled with either a localized or general European recession, could easily multiply national strains and pressures which might stall the Community, reduce its pace, or reverse its direction.

Political support for the Community, sustained over the years by the popularity or power of de Gaulle and Adenauer, may weaken as new European leaders rise to power. The Community has still to face its severest internal stresses as its revolutionary economic and social changes take effect. These uncertainties, coupled with the insecurity generated by Soviet foreign policy, impel the Common Market forward in a search for increased central resources, accepted codes of action, and institutions to meet the crises and tests that lie ahead.

IV   *The Larger European Community*

W<small>ITH</small> the establishment of the Common Market, the European movement swiftly condensed into two major streams, each pursuing its separate course amid tortuous efforts to bring both together. These efforts, involving an interplay of many internal and external forces, sought to carry forward the traditions of European cooperation built during the period of postwar reconstruction.

THE OEEC PRECEDENT

It will be recalled that Western Europe reacted to the Marshall Plan by forming the Organization for European Economic Cooperation (OEEC) to administer American aid. Joint scrutiny of the individual needs of member countries in the allocation of this aid established enduring habits of close consultation. The United States and Canada participated in the activities of the OEEC as associate members. The success of this unique organization in facilitating recovery paved the way for Western Europe's further rapid growth and development.

Two achievements of the OEEC, in particular, merit mention: the liberalization of quantitative controls on trade between members, and the restoration of convertibility of Europe's principal currencies. A system of liberalization percentages was used to remove quantitative restrictions on imports. With 1948 adopted as a reference year, member countries agreed to free products from quantitative import restrictions according to a given percentage of all imports during the reference year. The OEEC fixed the percentage to be freed successively at 50 percent in December 1949, 60 percent in September 1950, and 75 percent in February 1951. The percentage was further raised to 90 percent in 1955. This was eventually achieved, and in some cases exceeded, by nearly all OEEC countries.

Trade requires financing, however, and European reserves had been exhausted by the war. It was obvious to OEEC planners that trade liberalization would have to be accompanied by a reconstitution of Western Europe's monetary system. This was achieved through intra-European payments agreements, adopted in 1948 and 1949, and the European Payments Union (EPU), established in July 1950. The EPU functioned as a clearing house for the handling of payments arising from trade between OEEC members, performing services somewhat similar to the clearing transactions of the Federal Reserve system in the United States. A Bank for International Settlements (BIS) acted as the agent for the Payments Union, calculating every month each country's net balance for the previous month with the EPU (i.e., the member countries as a whole).

The BIS, on the last working day of the month, would convert each member country's bilateral balance with each of its partners into a unit of account equivalent to one United States dollar. Any debit balance of a member country with some of its partners would automatically be set off against its credit balances with others. Its net position with the EPU would then be settled either by payment to the Union or by drawing down its balance with the Union within the limits of a fixed quota of reserves. The EPU had access to $350 million in capital, made available at the outset by the United States, to enable it to make its monthly gold or dollar payments.

The European Payments Union proved itself an indispensable instrument in the rebuilding of Europe's financial structure. By the end of 1958, seven countries (Belgium, France, Germany, Italy, Luxembourg, the Netherlands, and the United Kingdom) concluded that their currencies were sufficiently strong to have their convertibility restored. Most of the other OEEC countries soon followed suit, and for the first time in almost three decades Europe's major currencies were free of the tangle of bilateral payments agreements.

These and other cooperative efforts played a major role in strengthening the economic foundations of Western Europe as a whole. This very strength, however, also made possible the rise of regional economic groups sufficiently vigorous to give expression to the undercurrents of rivalry within the European movement. For a time, the OEEC provided a natural framework within which its member nations sought to resolve the trading differences and difficulties that emerged with the formation of the Common Market. Intensive and exhausting negotiations during 1957 and 1958 soon demonstrated that the differences went deeper than mere questions of trade and beyond the capabilities of the OEEC to resolve. The OEEC had functioned well as long as it could count on substantial agreement among participating countries on fundamental purposes, objectives, and approaches to Western Europe's long-term problems. The fear and distrust greeting the birth of the European Economic Community revealed that such agreement no longer existed.

THE EFTA RESPONSE

As noted in Chapter 1, seven non-Common Market countries—the United Kingdom, Norway, Denmark, Sweden, Switzerland, Austria, and Portugal—responded to the creation of the EEC by forming in 1959 the European Free Trade Association (EFTA). Significantly, the EFTA agreement took the form of a convention, rather than a treaty, to emphasize that its scope was more limited and narrower than that of the European Economic Community (see Figure 3). It shared with the Treaty of Rome the objective of eliminating tariffs and quotas among members, but made no provision for a common external tariff. As a free trade area rather than a customs union, the EFTA permitted each member to keep its autonomy in setting its own tariffs against nonmembers and lacked the elaborate machinery of the EEC.

Though economically less powerful than the Six, the Seven con-

FIGURE 3

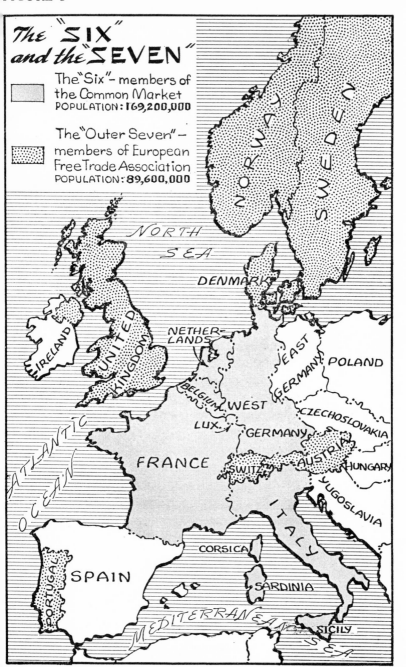

The "SIX" and the "SEVEN"

The "Six" – members of the Common Market
POPULATION: 169,200,000

The "Outer Seven" – members of European Free Trade Association
POPULATION: 89,600,000

NORTH SEA

NORWAY

SWEDEN

DENMARK

IRELAND

UNITED KINGDOM

NETHER-LANDS

BELGIUM

LUX.

WEST GERMANY

EAST GERMANY

POLAND

CZECHOSLOVAKIA

AUSTRIA

SWITZ.

HUNGARY

ATLANTIC OCEAN

FRANCE

ITALY

YUGOSLAVIA

SPAIN

PORTUGAL

CORSICA

SARDINIA

MEDITERRANEAN SEA

SICILY

stituted a substantial economic bloc, with 90 million people, the resources of the British Commonwealth, and a combined export-import trade almost three-fourths as large as that of the Common Market. Its total national income was about two-thirds that of the EEC. The United Kingdom contributed the predominant share of that income as well as 60 percent of the group's population.

The preamble of the EFTA Convention set forth the basic objective of the Association: to eliminate barriers to trade between member countries in order to promote in each a sustained expansion of economic activity, full employment, increased productivity and the rational use of resources, financial stability, and continuous improvement of living standards. A supplementary resolution affirmed the EFTA's determination to seek the removal of barriers to world trade in general, and to promote closer economic cooperation with the Common Market countries and among all eighteen member nations of the OEEC.

A Council was the only permanent organization provided for in the Convention. As both the administrative and consultative organ of the Association, it was charged with the general supervision of the activities of the group. It comprised one representative from every member state, each of whom had one vote. Decisions were to be made on the basis of unanimity except in certain specified cases.

With the objective of removing obstacles to trade in industrial products, the Convention established a timetable for the reduction of tariffs corresponding roughly to that of the Common Market, beginning with an original reduction of 20 precent on July 1, 1960, and followed by successive 10 percent reductions until all tariffs are abolished. The initial target date for achieving this goal was 1970. Each member country was allowed to reduce its tariffs on imports from other EFTA countries at a faster rate if it wished. The entire schedule of reductions could be accelerated if desired by all members.

To meet the problem of goods not originating within the Association, three "rules of origin" were spelled out. In order to qualify for tariff reduction and eventual elimination, goods must either:

1) have been wholly produced within the area of the EFTA, (2) have been produced by certain specified processes, or (3) must consist, in no less than 50 percent of their export value, of materials or parts originating within the area. In determining the composition of goods under the "percentage rule," the Convention included a rather extensive list of primary products and raw materials which could be considered to have originated within the free trade area, even though they might actually be imported from outside. This was to insure that the exports of the primary producing countries outside the free trade area would not suffer unduly.

The Convention also dealt with the removal of quantitative restrictions on both imports and exports—including quotas, licensing regulations, and other administrative practices. The timetable established for eliminating import barriers followed closely the schedule set out for the removal of tariffs. Export barriers of a quantitative nature were to be removed by January 1962 at the latest. Exceptions were limited to cases which were internationally recognized as justifying special treatment—such as protection of public morals and human, plant, or animal health, and safeguarding national treasures.

Among the more important provisions of the Convention were a number of articles dealing with "rules of competition" designed to insure that the beneficial effects of reduced trade barriers would not be nullified by other kinds of restrictions.

Specifically, the Convention proscribed direct export subsidies, exchange controls which give preferential treatment to exporters, the remission of direct taxes or other charges which have the same effect, and the extension of below-cost government export credits. In addition, it prohibited monopolistic agreements by private or public entities and included provisions against "dumping" or subsidizing imports.

A number of provisions touched on "invisible" transactions, such as the movement of investment capital and dividend payments. They contained few directives for liberalization on the grounds that arrangements for consultation on such matters were available through other channels. The Convention stated specifically that the members of the Association were not to be exempt from their obligations to the OEEC, the International Monetary Fund, and the General Agreement on Tariffs and Trade (GATT). The Convention recognized that internal financial and economic policies of member states can and do affect other members, and permitted the Council, by unanimous decision, to make recommendations concerning them.

Three specific escape clauses, finally, were incorporated in the Convention. These dealt with national security, balance of payments difficulties, and difficulties in particular sectors of member countries' economies. Members were given broad authority to invoke the first but in applying the second and third were required to inform the Council. By majority vote, the Council could make recommendations designed to assist the invoking country and its partners in finding a solution to the problem at issue.

The division of Europe's principal traders into two groups aroused fears, particularly in the United States, that deeply rooted European discords would simply be perpetuated. Although both blocs were committed to more liberal trade patterns, the varied attitudes and policies adopted in pursuit of this objective raised the danger of severe economic dislocations and political disunity.

THE SEARCH FOR A NEW FRAMEWORK: THE OECD

The United States, though more sympathetic to the EEC than to the EFTA, sought to enlist both blocs in a new cooperative venture that would transcend their division. Economic and political considerations intertwined to intensify American concern with the direction of European affairs. The trade division in Europe discriminated against countries who were members of neither bloc; underscored the vulnerable interdependence of the industrialized economies of Europe and North America; hampered the ability of the free world to respond concertedly to the needs of less developed countries; and weakened the West in the face of the ramified challenges posed by Soviet power. It became vital, from the American perspective, that the problems between the Six and Seven be worked out within some transatlantic framework that would project the interests of third countries and provide a greater measure of equilibrium, stability, and resilience to the tangled skein of international economics.

With these objectives in mind, the United States recommended a reconstitution of the OEEC in late 1959. The heads of Government of the United States, France, Germany, and the United Kingdom officially endorsed a study of methods to promote consultations on major economic problems in December of that year. The following January, the Foreign Ministers of the 18 OEEC members and the United States and Canada (associate members) named a group of four experts to determine means by which the 20 nations could improve their cooperation. The experts' report, published in April 1960, proposed that the OEEC be remodeled into the Organization for Economic Cooperation and Development (OECD) with Canada and the United States as full members. A new convention with related protocols was signed in December 1960 by the Ministers of the 20 governments. The United States Senate gave its advice and consent to ratification of the Convention on March 16, 1961.

Among the many hopes that underpinned United States support of the OECD was an expectation that the new organization would perform a vital educational function—impressing Americans with the delicately balanced economic interdependence of the West, and imbuing European leaders with a better understanding of the urgent need for foreign aid to encourage the development of newly independent countries. These considerations played a major role in securing United States Senate approval of the OECD Convention. The Senate Foreign Relations Committee, for example, declared the following in reporting its recommended approval:

> The American experience with foreign aid must be brought to bear upon the consciousness of other capital exporting countries. Bilateral talks, even if conducted at the White House level, are no substitute for an education that can spread

throughout the OECD membership by joint exposure to the same information, to the philosophy and logic that have motivated American foreign aid from the beginning.

If Europeans have not developed a keen appreciation for foreign aid, it is also true that Americans have been laggard in acknowledging the economic interdependence of the Atlantic Basin countries. The truth is that the West can no longer tolerate economic disequilibrium. Too much depends on the vigor of its interdependent economy, greater by far than the sum of the individual parts.

More important than the collective GNP ($775.5 billion) of the OECD members are the scientific and technical resources upon which it is built. With the OECD, these resources can be mobilized and directed toward productive purposes. For the first time, a group of countries with common interests, beset by common problems, will be free to discuss their goals and problems within an organization designed for precisely that purpose.[1]

The United States also hoped that the OECD, by emphasizing Europe's broader involvement in the problems of free-world development, would facilitate the reconciliation of the Six and the Seven. As an umbrella embracing both groups, the new organization could prevent hardening of vested interests in the existing fragmentation. In the American view, the emergence of a dual Europe underscored the need for a larger forum at once embracing and transcending the immediate interests of both the Common Market and the European Free Trade Association. Such a forum would fulfill a number of purposes: act as an outside "conscience" for the two European groupings; serve as a framework for continued discussions with all European nations, including those left out of both bloc; and provide the industrialized West with common goals and

[1] "Organization for Economic Cooperation and Development." Report of the Committee on Foreign Relations, United States Senate, on Executive E, 87th Congress, 1st Session, March 8, 1961, p. 14.

procedures for meeting the pressing problems of the primary producing countries, the underdeveloped areas, and the low-cost competition countries of Asia and the Orient.

A transformed OEEC seemed to offer the best hope for fulfilling
these purposes. It came closest to the proposed forum in terms of
size and experience. It had done much to help coordinate and
accommodate nations' fiscal and monetary policies. It possessed a
core of experienced international civil servants as well as the ability
to conduct vitally needed technical studies. Its give-and-take procedures had built over the years an unwritten common code of
civilized international behavior. Although it had increasingly come
to function in a state of suspended animation, largely because of
rapid economic changes and Western Europe's divisions, it continued to possess invaluable resources. Transfigured with a new and
broader orientation, it held out the hope of enabling the West to
meet more effectively the new needs of Europe, the larger Atlantic
community, and the free world as a whole.

Accordingly, the Organization for Economic Cooperation and
Development (OECD), built upon the institutional framework,
procedural experience, and membership of the OEEC, was assigned
new, broader objectives (though fewer and less demanding obligations). The OEEC, as indicated, had concerned itself mainly with
European recovery and with regional trade-and-payments arrangements. Members had bound themselves to various rules and obligations, such as the code of liberalization for removing quantitative
restrictions on imports within a system of reciprocal commitments.
The broad purposes of the OECD, on the other hand, were to promote economic stability and orderly growth of the economies of
member countries, devise more effective methods for assisting less
developed countries on an equitable basis, and contribute to the expansion of world trade. Instead of codes and obligations, the OECD
Charter provided for consultation and voluntary cooperation. Its
essential function was to serve as a forum for exchanging information and viewpoints, encouraging the coordination of economic

policies of member countries, and reaching agreement on methods to deal with balance-of-payments and other problems endangering stability in free-world economic relations. The OECD was not established as a "closed" organization, but was open for additional members as well as for liaison with other regional groupings. Members of the EEC were given the option of acting individually within the OECD, or jointly through one of their commissions.

European countries supported the formation of the OECD with mixed emotions. Increased cooperation with the United States was welcomed. There was broad agreement that the aims of the new organization—economic growth, expanded trade, expanding aid —were the right ones for the coming decade. But neither the Seven nor the Six viewed the OECD as an adequate substitute for a closer arrangement with each other. Both believed that the United States would be more reluctant than its European partners to undertake commitments subjecting its domestic policies to international scrutiny and judgment. There was doubt that the process of global tariff reduction could be carried very far without substantial reciprocal tariff cuts by the United States, yet this seemed unlikely in view of various limiting provisions in existing American trade-agreements legislation, which permitted little room for maneuver and bargaining.

Perhaps more important, there was considerable disappointment in Europe that the OECD would be somewhat weaker than its predecessor, despite the new "global" orientation. The OEEC had enjoyed executive power to the extent that its unanimous decisions were binding on all its members and had the force of law. Shorn of this power, the OECD appeared to promise little more than "cooperation by candlelight." In a sense, its formation only brought out the division of Europe into sharper relief by replacing an existing European link with a weaker transatlantic one. By the same token, however, the dissolution of the OEEC intensified the pressure on both European blocs to find an independent solution to their differences.

THE HARDENING OF DIVISIONS

By 1961, both the EFTA and the EEC could point to significant progress toward developing their separate programs. In both groups, tariffs were coming down ahead of schedule. The EEC countries were coming to grips with many of the more difficult problems of economic integration, and the EFTA began to study problems of agricultural trade. Each group was enlarged by the addition of its first new associate: Finland signed a treaty of association with the EFTA early in March, and Greece reached agreement with the EEC later the same month. While neither of these countries became a full member of its group, both were prepared to participate in most of the tariff reductions required of members.

Finland's agreement with the EFTA permitted termination of the association on three months' notice by either party. A joint council separate from the EFTA Council of Ministers was set up to administer the agreement since Finland could not, as an associate, take part in the EFTA institutions or their meetings to consider concerted policy. In view of trade agreements with the Soviet bloc, Finland continued to apply quotas against EFTA members on several products, such as oil, coal, and fertilizers. The Seven and Finland agreed, however, to eliminate all tariffs among themselves by 1970.

For Greece, the door was at least open for eventual full membership in the Common Market. The agreement with the EEC established a customs union that permitted a slower timetable than the customs union of the Six. On most products, internal tariffs would be cut to zero over a 12-year period, while for others the transition period would take 22 years. Of more immediate importance, the agreement provided Greece with $125 million in credits to be extended over a period of five years by the Common Market's European Investment Bank.

In both economic camps, tariff cutting provided the most obvious signs of internal progress. The Community's third 10 percent reduction in internal trade barriers went into effect at the beginning of 1961. The Ministerial Council of the Seven agreed in February to make EFTA's next 10 percent internal tariff cut effective the following July, six months ahead of schedule. Members of EFTA also agreed to study the possibility of further acceleration of their timetable for tariff cuts, to review their schedule for eliminating quotas on industrial goods, and to complete a study of ways to encourage agricultural trade among themselves. Although the EFTA, unlike the EEC, had no requirement to work out a common agricultural policy, the move toward cooperation in this difficult field was accepted as an important test of EFTA's viability in the absence of formal treaty obligations.

In the Common Market, trade liberalization did not proceed without some strain. Alleged violations of the Rome Treaty—Italy was accused of levying excessive duties on radio tubes and suspending imports of pork products from other EEC countries—were for the first time pressed in court. The complaints affected only a very small portion of Common Market trade, but provided a significant test of the Community's ability to enforce rules laid down in the treaty. In general, however, the business community of the Six represented a strong element of support for the movement toward internal free trade. Most European firms, instead of fighting tariff cuts, modernized and reorganized to prepare themselves for the end of the transition period. The continued high level of spending for new plant and equipment by EEC firms, and the large number of mergers and new partnerships, reflected considerable planning ahead for the time when tariffs and quotas would be eliminated.

Significantly, French and Italian manufacturers, after two years of tariff cutting, displayed a subtle but rapid change in their attitude toward protection. Traditionally fearful that they would not be able to compete in a free market, they emerged as leaders in expansion of markets in other EEC members. On many items, French tariffs were reduced unilaterally in 1961 by 5 to 10 percent. Most of these cuts were extended to countries outside the Community, including the United States. This change in attitude did much to ease acceptance of the Common Market's accelerated schedule of tariff reductions. An extra 10 percent cut set for the end of 1961 brought internal tariffs down to 50 percent of their pre-EEC level—three full years ahead of the schedule provided by the Rome Treaty.

Other problems in the program of economic integration encountered more difficulty. The EEC Commission's proposals for a common antitrust policy, requiring that most inter-company agreements be registered in advance with the Commission, ran into the stiff opposition of business representatives in the Common Market's Economic and Social Committee. In the field of agriculture, wide differences of opinion continued to prevent agreement among the Six on the extent to which—and how rapidly—agricultural trade should be freed of restrictions. With substantial Dutch and French support, the Commission advocated removing most of the barriers to the free flow of farm products within the Community. Farmers in each member country, however, exerted powerful political pressure to maintain the systems of protection that had existed for close to a century. In some countries, particularly Germany, there was growing recognition that national protection was on the way out, but also a feeling that the process should permit gradual improvement in national agricultural efficiency.

Despite such great difficulties, Community members could look look back at their performance with confidence that their efforts to stimulate the flow of goods were working well. In 1960, the Six enjoyed a 25 percent increase in trade among themselves over 1959. The gain in 1959 over 1958 was 19 percent. Imports from outside the Common Market in 1960 went up about 22 percent over the preceding year, with imports from the United States rising by more than 50 percent. By way of contrast, trade among EFTA members in 1960 increased by about 15 percent. While much of the increase in European trade would have occurred in any event as a result of general industrial growth, it appeared that the framework of economic regionalism provided an additional stimulus. The gains in trade between the Six and the Seven were also large, but not as impressive as those within each bloc.

PRESSURES FOR RECONCILIATION

As the Six and Seven pushed the development of their own organizations, pressure for agreement mounted inside each group. Businessmen, concerned about a loss of markets in the other group, represented an important source of this pressure in both the EEC and the EFTA countries. Members of the Seven faced increasing tariff disadvantages at the very time that the Continent appeared to offer the greatest potential for market growth. The Common Market countries, though less dependent on trade with the Seven, faced similar anxieties.

From time to time, various plans had been proposed to reduce tariff discrimination between the two groups. These plans, however, had concentrated on the commercial differences between the Six and the Seven, and had failed to come to grips with the root of the "split." But during 1961 there appeared a greater willingness to admit that the most important obstacle to a commercial agreement between the EEC and the EFTA was the difference in their approach to European unity. This difference was succinctly capsuled by one report as follows:

> One way of putting it is that EEC has started with a written constitution, requiring the member countries to cooperate; while EFTA has started with a general statement of intention, and prefers to let its constitution grow naturally—as did the British constitution—to fit the needs of member countries as they evolve.[2]

It became increasingly apparent that the economic differences separating the two groups were not insoluble, but could be resolved if the differences in approach to integration were bridged.

That this still presented great difficulties was underscored by the diversity and conflict that continued to mark the general climate of Western European opinion.

[2] The Chase Manhattan Bank. "EEC and EFTA in 1961 in *Report on Western Europe,* No. 12, March-April 1961, p. 4.

French attitudes reflected a substantial bias against British policies. The feeling lingered that the United Kingdom was out to block the Common Market. The EFTA tended to be viewed as an artificial entity, forced on the smaller members by Great Britain. This view was coupled with a reluctance to consider any special arrangements with the EFTA on the basis that the blocs represented irreconcilable basic ideas. Other factors inhibiting the emergence of latent interest in a broader outlook were the priority placed on French-German intimacy and urgent internal problems— Algeria, pressures from French agriculture and protected segments of French industry, potential agricultural competiton from Greece and Turkey, and various adjustments to the effects of the Common Market.

German attitudes were colored by the fact that Germany exported far more to the EFTA than to its partners in the Common Market. Some officials, particularly Economic Minister Erhard, had long hoped to broaden Germany's economic relations with all nations, including the free trade area, with a minimum reliance on the apparatus of institutions. The United Kingdom was respected and the Commonwealth's importance to the free world appreciated. Many German governmental, political, and business leaders favored closer links with the EFTA. They appeared determined to come to a solution in time, but showed no strong sense of urgency. Concerned more with the Common Market's political rather than purely economic implications, Germany was anxious not to endanger its greatest achievement—the termination of French-German enmity. At the same time, however, an important segment of German opinion considered the unification of Germany more important than the general goals of European integration.

Italy was perhaps the most "outward looking" of the EEC countries. Non-Community markets received half of Italy's exports. Italians wanted better arrangements with the EFTA and, along with Benelux, a stronger voice in the forum of the EEC. Support for maintaining an open door to Britain stemmed in part from a desire to check the dominance of France and Germany in Continental affairs.

The countries associated with the United Kingdom in the EFTA also had substantial economic interests in both blocs. Their preference for the free-trade area rested on such factors as reluctance to prejudice their industries in third countries by raising outer tariffs; fear of cheap labor; memories of past German ambitions; unwillingness to join a grouping which might be dominated by France; and historic and trade ties with Great Britain. Nevertheless, these countries were concerned about a hardening of vested interests in a division and wanted to see some Europe-wide association or Atlantic grouping take shape. They were worried, however, that Britain might make a separate arrangement with the EEC which would ignore their interests.

Britain itself was undergoing painful internal psychological adjustments. United Kingdom attitudes were still influenced by feelings that Britain's maritime destiny set it apart from Europe, as in the Churchillian phrase: "Each time we must choose between Europe and the open sea, we shall always choose the open sea." Historic and emotional ties to the Commonwealth remained strong. To this pull was added the attraction of maintaining a special relationship with the United States which would permit Britain to remain independent of the Continent and at the same time serve as an intermediary between the United States and Europe. Memories of Britain's former position, prestige, and power—enabling it to move into or away from the European scene and to maintain a political balance agreeable to it—continued to exert an influence.

Increasingly, however, British policymakers and opinion leaders acknowledged the unreality of former conceptions of greatness. There was growing awareness that traditional symbols of sovereignty could not preserve the substance of power and influence. The Commonwealth no longer served as a reservoir of strength and united political support. The United States had made it plain that it could not recognize any special relationship with Britain outside a European context.

Clearly, the Seven's informal cooperative approach to economic integration could not match the energetic and imaginative drive of the EEC. Britain's growing balance-of-payments problems and need to increase exports only emphasized its economic vulnerability. The rise of Asian-African solidarity and the diminishing importance of the Commonwealth preference system argued strongly for a closer relationship between the United Kingdom and other European countries. In sum, it appeared that Britain could not long maintain an adequate rate of growth unless it became a partner in Europe's new economic complex, and that, in political terms, Britain could only remain an important world power if it joined the new "superpower."

Thus, British thinking turned more and more to a concern with both the political and economic risks of staying out of Europe. Despite a profound reluctance to hand over to some outside constitutional body the traditional prerogatives of sovereignty, British leaders began to realize that political purposes of the Common Market could not be blunted and that Britain, to survive, would have to share in the life and dynamic outlook of Europe. In the words of a Continental European: "Either the United Kingdom will be in Europe, or there will be a Europe united against the United Kingdom."

But equally important as an influence on changing British attitudes was the consideration that the Common Market's ultimate political development, while still clouded with uncertainty, might take forms less supranational than had been originally feared. Signs within the EEC pointed to a gradual shift of power away from the Commission and toward the Council of Ministers and the member states, particularly France and Germany. The trend of developments appeared to emphasize intergovernmental cooperation rather than the movement toward federation. General de Gaulle's views on the right road to unity in Europe worked as a major force in this direction. Vigorously propounded at a Paris press conference in the fall of 1960, these views deeply influenced the outlook for developing European relationships and merit full quotation:

To build Europe, that is to say, to unite it, is evidently some-thing essential. It is trite to ask why this great center of civiliza-tion, of strength, of reason, of prosperity is being smothered by its own ashes. All that is necessary, in such a domain, is to pro-ceed, not by following our dreams, but according to realities.

Now, what are the realities of Europe? What are the pillars on which it can be built? The States are, in truth, certainly very different from one another, each of which has its own spirit, its own history, its own language, its own misfortunes, glories and ambitions; but these States are the only entities that have the right to order and the authority to act. To imagine that something can be built that would be effective for action and that would be approved by the people outside and above the States—this is a dream.

Of course it is true that, while waiting to come to grips with Europe's problem and tackle it as a whole, it has been possible to institute certain organs that are more or less extranational. These organs have their technical value, but they do not have, they cannot have authority and, consequently, political effec-tiveness. As long as nothing serious happens, they function without much difficulty, but as soon as a tragic situation appears, a major problem to be solved, it can then be seen that one 'High Authority' or another has no authority over the vari-ous national categories and that only the States have it. This is what was proved not long ago with regard to the coal crisis, and it is what may be seen with regard to the Common Market when there are problems of agricultural products and economic aid to be furnished to the African States or of the relations be-tween the Common Market and the free trade area.

Once again, it is quite natural that the States of Europe have at their disposal specialized organs for the problems that they have in common, in order to help formulate and, if need be, fol-low up their decisions; but the right to take these decisions is theirs alone. To ensure regular cooperation between the States of Western Europe is what France considers as desirable, possible and practical in the political, economic, and cultural domains and in that of defense.

This requires organized, regular consultation between responsible Governments, and then the work of specialized organs in each of the common domains which are subordinate to the Governments. This requires periodic deliberations by an assembly formed of delegates from the national parliaments, and in my opinion, this will have to require, as soon as possible, a formal European referendum so as to give this launching of Europe the character of popular support and initiative that is indispensable.

As it happens the States of Europe have at present between them, in common, great means of action and also, very great problems. As it happens their former enmities are being reduced to minor proportions. In short, as it happens, the opportunity is at hand. Certainly, if this course is taken, if one can hope that we shall embark on it, ties will be increased and habits will take shape. Then, as time does its work, little by little, it is possible that new steps will be taken toward European unity.[3]

Britain devoted many months to assessing the impact and implications of this public declaration. De Gaulle's position provided enough common ground to permit serious British consideration of very far-reaching arrangements with the Six, including membership in the EEC. More importantly, the Gaullist attitude made clear that the United Kingdom still had the opportunity, if it wished to work with the "Europeans," to help resolve the crucial question of Western Europe's ultimate political construction. The emergence of a new willingness by the British Government to consider joining the Common Market was accompanied by more earnest efforts to explore technically workable solutions to the economic problems previously used for the tactical purpose of raising objections to such membership.

[3] Ambassade de France, Service de Presse et D'Information, New York. Speeches and Press Conferences, No. 152, September 5, 1960, pp. 8-9.

Britain's current negotiations with the EEC reflect both the decline of British influence in Europe and a recognition of the conditions necessary to retain such influence. The problems in coming to terms with the Common Market are serious. Beyond economic difficulties involving the EFTA, the Commonwealth, and the British colonies is the fundamental issue of joining Europe's political destiny. This step is being approached with the caution that comes from an awareness of being on the threshold of an irrevocable turning point in history.

V *Outlook and Implications*

THE long-term outlook for European unity is col‐
ored by barriers to unification which may prove as persistent as the
efforts to overcome them. These barriers basically are not rooted in
the division of Western Europe into rival trading blocs.

As pointed out by Professor Emile Benoit in his admirable study,
Europe At Sixes and Sevens, the necessity to redirect a fraction of
one's trade to new markets may involve some difficult adjustments,
but is scarcely a tragedy. According to expert reports, for example,
the United Kingdom, as a result of anticipated trade diversion,
would have lost no more than 1 to 3 percent of the approximately
14 percent of its exports that went to the EEC. In short, the split be‐
tween the Six and the Seven did not create any long-lasting di‐
visions or political hostilities which were not already in existence.

BRITAIN'S DILEMMAS

Most candid observers, British or otherwise, today recognize
freely that Britain's reluctance to join the Common Market had
stemmed largely from traditional and political considerations. It is
difficult to give overriding importance to any one of these consider‐
ations, since all of them have long influenced British thinking.

Certainly, traditional British policy toward the Continental
powers—a policy which was effectively pursued throughout the
nineteenth century—occupies an important position in the over-all
picture. The main elements in this policy were (1) to prevent any
one single power from dominating the Continent and (2) to keep a
bridgehead on the Continent by keeping the low countries free
from domination by their more powerful neighbors. A third

element was added to these during the first half of this century: a latent mistrust of the three main Continental powers because of their manifest inability to develop stable and democratic political structures.

Traditionally, Britain would have responded to any development such as the Common Market by organizing a rival grouping strong enough to break it up. It goes without saying, however, that the conditions which might have made such a reaction valid in the nineteenth century no longer existed. Although Britain emerged from World War II as the strongest of the Western European powers, its relative ability to influence world power relationships was greatly reduced, both because of the disintegration of the Empire and because of the emergence of the United States and the Soviet Union as the principal contenders for world leadership. Further, of course, the principal threat to British security now came not from its former antagonists in Western Europe, but from beyond the Elbe, and modern weaponry had reduced the distance from Moscow to London to an infinitely shorter expanse than existed between Dover and Dieppe in 1940.

Closely related to the traditional British position in Europe is the relationship which evolved between Britain and the United States, reaching a peak in the formation of the Atlantic Alliance during World War II. It has been aptly said that "in British postwar policies, particularly economic ones, a certain nostalgia for the wartime partnership, or at least of the immediate postwar phase, when the British went to Bretton Woods with visions of a world economic order over which pound and dollar would preside side by side, has played a notable part." [1]

This is not to say that economic considerations are not vitally important. A serious problem influencing British policy centers on the differences between British and Continental agricultural policies. On the Continent, the Six generally maintain farm prices at a high level by import quotas and tariffs, with the consumer, in a sense,

[1] Christopher Layton. *Britain's European Dilemma.* London: European Youth Campaign, 1959, p. 6.

subsidizing the farmer through higher prices. In Britain, prices of farm products are lower, but the farmer's income is augmented by direct subsidy and other forms of aid, with the taxpayer bearing the burden. It is difficult to see how Britain can adapt to the Continental system without hurting the British farmer.

Political implications in this case are largely confined to domestic British politics. This issue has caused concern not only among the farmers and the British Labor Party, but also among some sectors of the Conservative Party. It has been estimated, for example, that joining the Common Market could lose the Conservative Party as many as 80 parliamentary seats in agricultural districts. The principal objection of Labor leaders stems from dismay at the prospect of higher food prices if the Continental system is adopted in Britain without considerable modification.

Another critical issue is the effect that joining the Common Market will have on the complex economic and political relationship between Britain and the Commonwealth. The contribution of Commonwealth ties to Britain's stature as a world power is difficult to measure, but real. Any move weakening these ties could also have a detrimental effect on Britain's political position. This factor, of course, must be weighed against the possible political gains resulting from British membership in the Common Market.

Intricately interwoven with these considerations is the question of how British entry into the Common Market will affect the trading relations binding the Commonwealth countries to Britain. Undoubtedly, the fear of disrupting Commonwealth trade has been used as an excuse by British statesmen to obscure their political objections to the Common Market—but an excuse containing considerably more than a few grains of truth. For while the political structure of the Commonwealth may be intangible and subject to strains, economic relations between its many parts are very real indeed.

A glance at some of the elements of this relationship will illustrate the point. According to 1959 figures, about one-third of total British foreign trade—both exports and imports—was with Commonwealth countries. Since about one-fifth of the total British Gross National Product (GNP) was generated from exports, this meant that between 7 and 8 percent of Britain's economy was linked to trade with the Commonwealth. As a rough comparison, this was almost twice the percentage that *total* United States exports contributed to the United States GNP. If the situation were reversed, the trade involved would have been the source of over 5 million jobs for American workers—a factor which policymakers could hardly overlook when considering measures which might radically alter the trade picture.

British trade is equally, if not more, important to the Commonwealth countries. About one-sixth of Canada's exports go to Britain, about one-third of those of India and Australia, and well over one-half of those of Nigeria and New Zealand. Most of these countries have enjoyed a preferential tariff position in the British market since 1932 through the imperial preference system.

British entry into the Common Market with no modification of the Common Market tariff structure would affect the Commonwealth trading system in three important ways: (1) Commonwealth goods would be denied their free entry to the United Kingdom; (2) they would receive worse treatment than comparable goods coming from the Common Market countries; and (3) the Commonwealth countries probably would be forced to deny Britain the preferences which some of its exports now receive. The most difficult problems would be faced by Commonwealth countries which rely on relatively few exports for their foreign exchange earnings and depend on free entry to the British market. This would be the case, for example, with wheat and dairy products from Canada, Australia, and New Zealand, with textiles from India, Pakistan, and Hong Kong, and with tropical products from Africa and the Caribbean.

It is clear that some accommodation will have to be made between Britain and the Six regarding the Commonwealth before Britain can enter the Common Market. Various proposals for reducing the painful effects of altering Britain's Commonwealth trading arrangements have been discussed. They include: modification of the present system of preferences between the Six and their overseas territories; granting of a series of tariff-free quotas for exports of the Commonwealth countries to Britain; reduction of barriers to Commonwealth goods in the Six to compensate for losses in exports to Britain; liberalization of the system of protection envisaged for Common Market agriculture; and introducing whatever modifications might be adopted gradually over a period of time. None of these measures is easy to implement. As Prime Minister Macmillan remarked: "A solution of the European economic problem cannot be reached without some losses and somebody being hurt somewhere."

COMMONWEALTH ATTITUDES
AND PROBLEMS OVERSEAS

Before announcing its decision to apply for Common Market membership, the British government was careful to explore the attitudes of the Commonwealth members. Early in July 1961 a team of three British cabinet ministers, promptly dubbed the "three missionaries" by the London press, were dispatched to every corner of the globe to discuss the proposition with Commonwealth leaders.

The purpose of their talks was two-fold: to gauge Commonwealth reaction to British application for Common Market membership, and to determine the conditions under which such application might be acceptable to individual Commonwealth countries, i.e., the extent to which Britain would have to protect their interests in negotiations with the Six.

This probing produced a number of surprises. Despite a great deal of general concern, New Zealand took a moderate view, even though its trade was expected to suffer more, perhaps, than that of any other country. In Australia, opposition was quite strong. The Australian government indicated it would want to conduct its own negotiations in the event that Britain decided to join the Six. Less opposition than expected was encountered among Commonwealth countries in Asia.

African countries, on the other hand, displayed more anxiety than anticipated, even though they were expected to be both short-run and long-run gainers if Britain linked itself with the Six. Ghana sent more than half of its cocoa to the Common Market countries, and Nigeria about one-third. Both faced a real danger in the tariff advantages enjoyed by other African countries associated with the EEC. President Nkrumah of Ghana informed the British that he would strongly object to Britain's joining the Six unless three conditions were met: Ghana should receive continued access to the British market, access to the European market on the same terms as the French territories, and developmental aid with no strings attached.

In Canada, objections came from an unexpected source. Canadians voiced concern less about the effects on their exports of wheat and raw material than about the long-term impact on their manufactured goods, which as yet comprise only a small fraction of total Canadian exports to Britain. In economic terms, the Canadian reaction perhaps best illustrates a general situation throughout the Commonwealth: almost all Commonwealth countries are in some stage of economic development. For the time being, their trading patterns with Britain are oriented toward an exchange of raw materials and foodstuffs for industrial goods. Eventually, however, they hope to have access to the British market for larger exports of manufactured goods. Any British move which might upset this pattern of development tends to be eyed with suspicion.

On the political side, nearly all Commonwealth countries initially expressed fear that British entry into the Common Market would weaken the structure of the Commonwealth, already shaken by the withdrawal of the Union of South Africa, and remove "the British influence" from the world. This sentiment was voiced especially strongly in Canada, but was also emphasized in Australia and the less developed areas of the Commonwealth, which looked to Britain for the protection of their interests in Europe and elsewhere.

Britain's overseas interests meet those of the Common Market most directly in Africa. Reflecting the division in Europe, independent Commonwealth countries find themselves pitted against formerly French, Belgian, and Italian territories now associated with the EEC. From a purely economic point of view, the association of African Commonwealth countries with an enlarged Common Market should not present great difficulties. The tropical products of the region do not compete with the agricultural commodities produced in Europe (as do the products of such countries as Australia, Canada, and New Zealand). Yet, as indicated, difficulties have arisen where least expected. Ghana, in particular, has branded the Common Market as another conspiracy of the West to keep the colonial peoples in bondage. Simultaneously, French-speaking African states have opposed Britain's moves toward the Continent so as not to share the advantages of the Common Market's external tariff with Commonwealth countries that had developed generally more advanced economies.

The rift in Africa is further complicated by the rise of rival political schools of thought contending for African leadership. Separate meetings, ostensibly to discuss plans for greater unity within Africa, were held in 1961 in Monrovia and Casablanca. The Monrovia group consisted of most of the French-speaking states with the addition of Nigeria, Liberia, and Sierra Leone and appeared to desire closer political and economic ties with the West. At Casablanca, Egypt, Morocco, and Algeria joined Guinea, Ghana, and Mali to consider their common future within a neutral or anti-Western framework. Nigeria, the largest and strongest of all the West African nations, could exert a key influence on the development and orientation of its neighbors. But whether a satisfactory relationship between Nigeria and the Common Market can reverse Africa's anti-Western direction remains an open question.

REORIENTATION OF NATIONAL POLICIES

Thus a wide spectrum of global economic and political issues find themselves intertwined in Western Europe's divisions. The strictly economic problems to be reconciled are great. In the final analysis, however, the fundamental obstacle to Western European solidarity is lodged in the political will of the individual states concerned. Technical objections and difficulties, basically, are insurmountable only to the extent that there is an unwillingness to remove them. The really deep-seated objections, frequently unstated, cannot be negotiated away without changes in basic national policies and attitudes.

Such changes are taking place, but it would be hazardous to predict their speed and final direction. In varying degrees, members of the EFTA have followed Britain's lead in welcoming some sort of link with the European integration movement. Norway and Denmark hope at the same time to maintain a common "Nordic" front with Sweden. In the case of Austria, Finland, Switzerland, and Sweden, traditions of neutrality or enforced isolation from the European movement argue against acceptance of the Common Market's political goals. The force of this argument may weaken with time, though the Soviet Union, through the demonstrated effect of its pressure on Finland, appears determined to prevent such an eventuality. Portugal may work for some tie-in with the Common Market as a less developed country along the lines of Greece or Turkey. Developments in countries not identified with the aspirations of either group—Ireland, Iceland, Spain, and perhaps even Yugoslavia—indicate a desire to become more closely associated with the main currents of European development.

Undoubtedly, the pattern of relationships that will finally emerge in Europe will be heavily influenced by the extent to which Britain, having turned its face to the Continent, will strive in earnest to develop the solidarity required by geography, history, and vital necessity. Prolonged and difficult negotiations are to be expected. For the EEC leaders, the spirit of the negotiations will be far more important than the technicalities involved. They are fearful that any quick admittance of new members or associates may endanger or weaken the political character of their Community. They are likely to defer any decisions pending a clearer demonstration of intent by outside applicants.

The United Kingdom is ready to go very far in accepting the

need for common action and, indeed, many of the economic features of the Rome Treaty. It remains to be seen to what extent this includes acceptance of the spirit and political overtones as well as the letter of the Treaty—to what extent the United Kingdom is prepared to participate not merely in a customs union, but in a new political and economic unit. It also remains to be seen whether the "Europeans" within the Community are willing to sacrifice the uncertain goal of a new federal state to a broader confederative arrangement which, though a revolutionary achievement in itself, would stop short of full political union.

Intensive bargaining will have to precede any true rapprochement between the EFTA countries and the EEC. Each of the Seven must overcome or circumvent special difficulties to bring negotiations with the Common Market to a successful conclusion. In the case of Switzerland, Austria, and Sweden, political considerations are dominant. These countries are willing to accept the economic obligations of the Rome Treaty and are certainly more able to do so than, for example, Greece or Turkey. They cannot, however, accept its political implications under current world conditions.

Different considerations apply to the United Kingdom, Denmark, and Norway. Here there is growing realization that new members would participate in the framing of Community policy, that the process would be gradual, that basic Community policies are still in their formative period, and that the eventual surrender of sovereignty in social and economic fields may be no greater than that already accepted in the military field through membership in NATO. Thus, assuming that the EEC finds Britain's political will to integrate with Europe acceptable, the main problems of negotiation may lie in the economic sphere. Chief among these are the need to protect Commonwealth interests and to find some feasible way of adapting the British system of direct agricultural subsidy to the common agricultural policy still to be evolved by the Community.

From Britain's point of view, eventual membership in the EEC would inevitably lead to major changes in the economy of the

United Kingdom to meet new and swiftly changing conditions. Many sectors of the domestic market which had enjoyed governmental protection would face sharp, new competition. On the other hand, the opening up of a vast and expanding mass market with a population approaching 270 million people would offer great new opportunities.

New circumstances would demand drastic adaptations by British trade and industry. But while the changes involved in joining the EEC can more or less be anticipated, the outlook if Britain were permanently excluded from the Community is dark and uncharted. Whatever the difficulties that joining would entail, the difficulties of staying out are likely to be larger and more threatening. This consideration, perhaps more than any other, can be expected to undergird the United Kingdom's new determination to reach an agreement with the EEC consistent with essential national interests and commitments.

ECONOMIC EFFECTS

The economic impact of the Common Market on the development of Europe as a whole and on the rest of the world, while expected to be profound, is difficult to assess (see Figure 4). Many of the basic decisions on trade and production structures, price levels, procedures, institutions, and internal adjustments have yet to be made. In greater or lesser degree, moreover, many of the economic trends accompanying the Common Market's growth would in all probability have occurred in any event. European economic development, in the absence of the Common Market, would still have been marked by increased American investments in Europe, more effective competition in some fields, diminished imports in others, and heightened productivity in others. A rapid expansion of Franco-German trade, British efforts to develop Continental markets, West German efforts to develop overseas markets, and a falling share of foods and crude materials in intra-Western European trade are tendencies which antedate the Common Market. There is no easy way to isolate and estimate the influence of the Rome

FIGURE 4

MAJOR WORLD ECONOMIC BLOCS, 1961

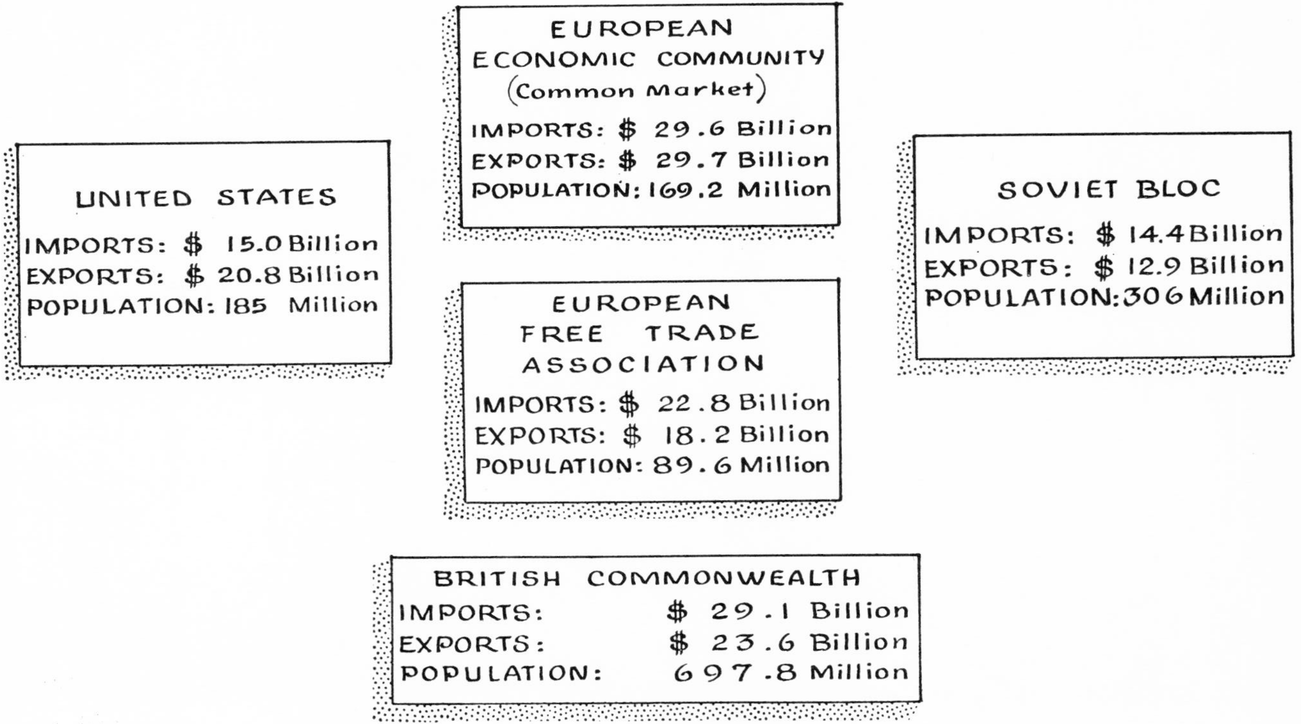

SOVIET BLOC

IMPORTS: $ 14.4 Billion
EXPORTS: $ 12.9 Billion
POPULATION: 306 Million

EUROPEAN
ECONOMIC COMMUNITY
(Common market)

IMPORTS: $ 29.6 Billion
EXPORTS: $ 29.7 Billion
POPULATION: 169.2 Million

EUROPEAN
FREE TRADE
ASSOCIATION

IMPORTS: $ 22.8 Billion
EXPORTS: $ 18.2 Billion
POPULATION: 89.6 Million

BRITISH COMMONWEALTH

IMPORTS: $ 29.1 Billion
EXPORTS: $ 23.6 Billion
POPULATION: 697.8 Million

UNITED STATES

IMPORTS: $ 15.0 Billion
EXPORTS: $ 20.8 Billion
POPULATION: 185 Million

Treaty itself. Materials for comprehensive impact analyses and studies are far from definitive.

On the basis of available information, however, students of the scene do not expect the Common Market to entail serious economic disadvantages for its individual members or for the rest of Europe. To a substantial degree, Western Europe trades with itself. The considerable trade which Common Market members carry on with other European countries is expanding, though not as rapidly as trade within the Community itself. A more dramatic shift in the pattern of intra-European trade could occur if the Western European economy as a whole fails to maintain its present rapid rate of growth.

Western European trade with Eastern Europe and the Soviet Union may increase as a result of Western Europe's general economic growth. Imports from the Eastern European area at present concentrate on foods, fuels, and raw materials. Prospects for increasing trade affecting basic chemicals, high-grade machinery, paper, and textiles are being explored actively. Political factors, however, enter heavily in the development of a common trade policy toward the communist bloc and may serve to restrain any rapid expansion of such trade.

The Soviet Union apparently hopes that a rising competitive struggle for markets between the advanced European industrial nations will produce growing pressure for more trade with communist countries. Western Europe's economic growth is producing some industrial surpluses which may well enhance the attractiveness of communist bloc trade offers. From the Soviet point of view, however, such trade is desirable because it would help relieve communist planning bottlenecks, contribute to Soviet industrial development, strengthen the communist ability to cut into capitalist markets, and weaken the Western alliance in the process. The Western nations, if they conclude that East-West trade can ultimately reap net advantage only for the communist bloc, may seek to establish a system of economic ground rules for meeting the potentially disruptive effects of communist state trading monopolies. Western

Europe's integration can be expected to facilitate any action taken in this direction.

The economic effects of European integration on the United States are likely to require various readjustments in the pattern of American overseas trade and investment. Some United States exports will face increasing competition as the opening of European mass markets stimulates more efficient internal production and distribution, and as competitive European industries strengthen themselves behind a protective tariff wall. At the same time, the increase in European purchasing power and consumer wants will open new opportunities for American exports of products which enjoy advantages in terms of research, design, and raw materials. United States investment in Europe is also likely to rise. To protect their existing markets and to share in the benefits of Europe's enlarged trading areas, a growing number of United States firms are establishing expatriated industries and subsidiaries to meet the demands of the European market. The extent to which American business can look to Europe for growing markets, however, will depend in large measure on the extent to which both sides of the Atlantic are serious in their intentions to liberalize trade policies.

The actual loss of American exports arising solely from EEC trade diversion is expected to be small and to affect chiefly manufactured and petroleum products. Professor Benoit estimates that the pressure of tariff differentials may endanger only about 5 to 10 percent of United States exports to the EEC (or about $120 million to $240 million worth of exports). The EFTA, by itself, would have an additional small impact. The two blocs combined, however, would expose a considerably larger number of United States products to intra-European competition and might raise the diversionary impact on American exports to a $400-$800 million range.

As demand in EEC countries expands and absorbs the capacities of Continental economies, the United States may find new openings for its exports in countries, such as Canada or Brazil, where European exports have been diverted to internal markets. On the other hand, increased Common Market activity in underdeveloped areas, particularly in South America and Africa, is expected to stimulate competition between the EEC and the United States for third markets. The mutual dependence of Western Europe and overseas primary-producing countries will remain substantial. Common Market needs for primary products offer relatively favorable prospects for countries exporting petroleum, basic metals, tropical foods, and beverages. Countries exporting agricultural raw materials or foodstuffs which compete directly with European production are less likely to enjoy a significant increase in sales to Western Europe.

Perhaps the most important economic gain to the United States resulting from European integration is to be found in the area of investment. The step-up in American investment in Europe since the formation of the EEC has already been tremendous. Between 1950 and 1959 the book value of United States direct investment in Europe had risen by about 200 percent, from $1.7 billion to $5.3 billion. The continued surge of such new investment is marked by the growth of "international" companies—drawing on varied national resources and talents without narrow ties to any particular national base—that may have a significant role to play in eroding the force of economic nationalism throughout the free world.

Apart from various commercial effects, the European experiment may also have a significant impact on United States domestic policies. Both the United States and Europe will have to cope with difficult problems of adjustment to new patterns of trade and industry. European successes and failures in re-training and re-locating workers, in spurring the development of depressed areas, in channeling investment, and in accommodating technological changes can be expected to influence the United States as it grapples with similar issues at home.

ULTIMATE IMPACT

In the larger perspective of history, the integration of Europe, hailed as the most significant innovation in Western statecraft since the formation of nation states, emerges as a momentous landmark in the development of the modern world. Nearly destroyed by forces of its own making, Europe is rising, phoenix-like, to provide fresh vitality to the civilization of which it has been at once the embodiment and driving force. As the Continent continues to unify in its own way to meet its own needs, creating new instrumentalities to deal with changing realities, it will alter irrevocably both the distribution of world power and the character of global relationships.

Within the framework of the Cold War, Western Europe's revival represents a serious blow to long-standing Soviet expectations and objectives. The capitalist West has not disintegrated to give way to a communist take-over. Instead, the communist leaders now confront a new and growing power combination. The campaign which the Soviet Union has mounted to obstruct the movement toward greater West European unity indicates the gravity of the threat to Soviet interests. In Britain, communist propaganda has warned that a merger with the Common Market would reduce the country to a satellite of France and Germany. The French have been urged to beware of British aspirations to dominate the Continent as well as of German military ambitions. Austria and Finland have been subjected to more direct intimidation (see Chapter 2). In underdeveloped countries, the Soviet Union has pictured a united Europe as a final betrayal and conspiracy by the West to thwart the legitimate aspirations of newly emerging nations.

Despite such efforts, the Soviet Union has been unable to conceal the collapse of its ideological cardhouse. The European Economic Community dramatically demonstrates that dynamic and creative progress is possible under free but self-disciplined institutions. The vitality of regional organization derives not only from its wider geographic coverage, permitting the harnessing of diverse human and material resources for the benefit of all, but also from its capacity to strengthen individual nations and governments. As these potentialities are realized—effectively destroying the illusion of Western decadence and paralysis—the free world may find new strength to cope with the convulsive revolutions—political, economic, social, demographic, technological, ideological—that have gripped this century.

By the same token, however, Europe's economic and political growth is likely to render the Continent increasingly less responsive to the leadership and influence of the United States. Superficially, this movement may take the form of stronger neutralist and third-force tendencies. More fundamentally, Europe will insist upon equal partnership, with all the attendant disagreements and strains, in dealing with external threats as well as with the larger problem of constructing a more healthy international environment. The United States, as it gradually loses its position of unquestioned dominance in the free world, will find it necessary to share with its allies ever more demanding, but hopefully less paralyzing, international responsibilities.

This long-term trend does not presage a real weakening of the bonds that gird the Atlantic Community of nations. Indeed, the spiritual cohesion of the West—in terms of commitments to common values and goals—may well be strengthened both within and beyond the Atlantic world. Eventually the foundations may be laid for the creation of a heterogeneous commonwealth of all free nations as a source of mutual consultation and moral and material support. But the number of voices that will expect influence in such a commonwealth will grow, as will disagreement and conflict on the specific policies and actions that must clothe the framework of common interests and objectives.

In any event, it is possible to foresee the rise, perhaps before the close of this century, of several integrated world blocs. Capturing the imagination of many underdeveloped areas, the example of Europe has done much to inspire integration plans in other areas. A Central American Common Market and a Latin American Free Trade Association have already been established by treaty. These ventures, ostensibly initiated for economic reasons, will encounter formidable economic hurdles due to the nature of the economies involved, but are likely to acquire considerable political potency in Latin American affairs. African nations are exploring the possibilities of establishing one or more common markets or free trade areas of their own. Similar projects are being considered by various countries in Southeast Asia. It may well be a matter of a few decades before mainland China, Latin America, and Africa join North America, the Soviet Union, and Europe as new centers of political influence.

Such a dispersed pattern of power—assuming that the free world as a whole maintains sufficient solidarity to foreclose indefinitely the prospects for further communist expansion—may itself ultimately resolve the attenuated East-West conflict. The drive for unity, paradoxically, is spurring a dynamic resurgence of pluralism in international relations. It is not only shattering the simple but explosive mold of bi-polarity established as a legacy of World War II, but shaping new techniques for diffusing and bridling power.

Perhaps the greatest hope, if not promise, of the institutional and procedural precedents now being forged in Europe is that modern man will succeed in finding new means for controlling the enormous power that threatens his troubled destiny on earth.

Selected Bibliography

Benoit, Emile. *Europe at Sixes and Sevens: The Common Market, the Free Trade Association, and the United States.* New York: Columbia University Press, 1961.

Camps, Miriam. *Division in Europe.* Policy Memorandum No. 21, Center of International Studies, Princeton University, June 15, 1960.

Committee for Economic Development, Research and Policy Committee. *The European Common Market and Its Meaning to the United States.* New York: 1959.

Dewhurst, J. Frederic, and John O. Coppock, P. Lamartine Yates, and Associates. *Europe's Needs and Resources: Trends and Prospects in Eighteen Countries.* New York: Twentieth Century Fund, 1961.

Economist Intelligence Unit, Ltd. *The Commonwealth and Europe.* London: 1961.

Foreign Policy Research Institute, University of Pennsylvania. *United States Foreign Policy in Western Europe.* Study No. 3 Prepared at the Request of the Committee on Foreign Relations, United States Senate. 86th Congress, 1st Session. Washington: U.S. Government Printing Office, 1959.

Frank, Isaiah. *The European Common Market.* New York: Frederick A. Praeger, Inc., 1961.

Freund, Gerald. *Germany Between Two Worlds.* New York: Harcourt, 1961.

Gunther, John. *Inside Europe Today.* New York: Harper & Brothers, 1961.

Morgan Guaranty Trust Company of New York. *Market Europe.* New York: 1961.

Scitovsky, Tibor. *Economic Theory and Western European Integration.* Stanford: Stanford University Press, 1958.

Tannenbaum, Edward R. *The New France*. Chicago: University of Chicago Press, 1961.

United States Congress. *A Study of European Economic Regionalism—A New Era in Free World Economic Politics*. Report of a Special Study Mission of the Subcommittee on Europe of the Committee on Foreign Affairs, United States House of Representatives. 86th Congress, 2d Session. Washington: U.S. Government Printing Office, 1960.

Woodhouse, C. M. *British Foreign Policy Since the Second World War*. London: Hutchinson, 1961.

Index